An Analysis of

Jonathan Riley-Smith's

The First Crusade and the Idea of Crusading

Damien Peters

www.macat.com
info@macat.com

Cover illustration: A. Richard Allen

Cataloguing in Publication Data
A catalogue record for this book is available from the British Library.
Library of Congress Cataloguing-in-Publication Data is available upon request.

ISBN 978-1-912302-74-1 (hardback)
ISBN 978-1-912128-25-9 (paperback)
ISBN 978-1-912281-62-6 (e-book)

Notice
The information in this book is designed to orientate readers of the work under analysis,
to elucidate and contextualise its key ideas and themes, and to aid in the development
of critical thinking skills. It is not meant to be used, nor should it be used, as a
substitute for original thinking or in place of original writing or research. References and
notes are provided for informational purposes and their presence does not constitute
endorsement of the information or opinions therein. This book is presented solely for
educational purposes. It is sold on the understanding that the publisher is not engaged
to provide any scholarly advice. The publisher has made every effort to ensure that
this book is accurate and up-to-date, but makes no warranties or representations with
regard to the completeness or reliability of the information it contains. The information
and the opinions provided herein are not guaranteed or warranted to produce particular
results and may not be suitable for students of every ability. The publisher shall not be
liable for any loss, damage or disruption arising from any errors or omissions, or from
the use of this book, including, but not limited to, special, incidental, consequential or
other damages caused, or alleged to have been caused, directly or indirectly, by the
information contained within.

CONTENTS

WAYS IN TO THE TEXT

Who Is Jonathan Riley-Smith?   9

What Does *The First Crusade* Say?   10

Why Does *The First Crusade* Matter?   12

SECTION 1: INFLUENCES

Module 1: The Author and the Historical Context   15

Module 2: Academic Context   19

Module 3: The Problem   24

Module 4: The Author's Contribution   28

SECTION 2: IDEAS

Module 5: Main Ideas   33

Module 6: Secondary Ideas   38

Module 7: Achievement   42

Module 8: Place in the Author's Work   46

SECTION 3: IMPACT

Module 9: The First Responses   51

Module 10: The Evolving Debate   56

Module 11: Impact and Influence Today   60

Module 12: Where Next?   64

Glossary of Terms   68

People Mentioned in the Text   77

Works Cited   83

THE MACAT LIBRARY

The Macat Library is a series of unique academic explorations of seminal works in the humanities and social sciences – books and papers that have had a significant and widely recognised impact on their disciplines. It has been created to serve as much more than just a summary of what lies between the covers of a great book. It illuminates and explores the influences on, ideas of, and impact of that book. Our goal is to offer a learning resource that encourages critical thinking and fosters a better, deeper understanding of important ideas.

Each publication is divided into three Sections: Influences, Ideas, and Impact. Each Section has four Modules. These explore every important facet of the work, and the responses to it.

This Section-Module structure makes a Macat Library book easy to use, but it has another important feature. Because each Macat book is written to the same format, it is possible (and encouraged!) to cross-reference multiple Macat books along the same lines of inquiry or research. This allows the reader to open up interesting interdisciplinary pathways.

To further aid your reading, lists of glossary terms and people mentioned are included at the end of this book (these are indicated by an asterisk [*] throughout) – as well as a list of works cited.

Macat has worked with the University of Cambridge to identify the elements of critical thinking and understand the ways in which six different skills combine to enable effective thinking.
Three allow us to fully understand a problem; three more give us the tools to solve it. Together, these six skills make up the **PACIER** model of critical thinking. They are:

ANALYSIS – understanding how an argument is built
EVALUATION – exploring the strengths and weaknesses of an argument
INTERPRETATION – understanding issues of meaning

CREATIVE THINKING – coming up with new ideas and fresh connections
PROBLEM-SOLVING – producing strong solutions
REASONING – creating strong arguments

To find out more, visit **WWW.MACAT.COM.**

CRITICAL THINKING AND *THE FIRST CRUSADE AND THE IDEA OF CRUSADING*

Primary critical thinking skill: EVALUATION
Secondary critical thinking skill: INTERPRETATION

Perhaps no work of history written in the 20th century has done more to undermine an existing consensus and cause its readers to re-evaluate their own preconceptions than has Jonathan Riley-Smith's revisionist account of the motives of the first crusaders. Riley-Smith's thesis – based on extensive original research and firmly rooted in his refusal to uncritically accept the evidence or reasoning of earlier historians – is that the majority of the men who travelled to the east on crusade in the years 1098-1100 were primarily motivated by faith. This finding, which ran directly counter to at least four centuries of consensus that other motives, not least greed for land, were more important, has helped to stimulate exciting reappraisals of the whole crusading movement. Riley-Smith backed it up with forensic examination of the key crusader-inspiring speech delivered by Pope Urban II, looking to clarify the meanings of five competing contemporary accounts in order to understand how an initially simple, and rather confused, appeal for help became a sophisticated rationale for the concept of 'just war.'

ABOUT THE AUTHOR OF THE ORIGINAL WORK

Born in 1938, British scholar **Jonathan Riley-Smith** was professor of ecclesiastical history at Cambridge, and was considered by many to be the greatest living historian of the Crusades. He revised and to some extent overturned the commonly held view that the medieval expeditions to conquer the Holy Lands were little more than fanatical acts of piracy and plunder. By using thorough traditional research methods allied to technological innovations, Riley-Smith reached the conclusion that there was also a significant spiritual side to these ventures. Driven by his passion for the subject, Riley-Smith helped found the Society for the Study of the Crusades and the Latin East. He died in 2016.

ABOUT THE AUTHOR OF THE ANALYSIS

Damien Peters holds an MA in the history of international relations from University College, Dublin.

ABOUT MACAT

GREAT WORKS FOR CRITICAL THINKING

Macat is focused on making the ideas of the world's great thinkers accessible and comprehensible to everybody, everywhere, in ways that promote the development of enhanced critical thinking skills.

It works with leading academics from the world's top universities to produce new analyses that focus on the ideas and the impact of the most influential works ever written across a wide variety of academic disciplines. Each of the works that sit at the heart of its growing library is an enduring example of great thinking. But by setting them in context – and looking at the influences that shaped their authors, as well as the responses they provoked – Macat encourages readers to look at these classics and game-changers with fresh eyes. Readers learn to think, engage and challenge their ideas, rather than simply accepting them.

'Macat offers an amazing first-of-its-kind tool for interdisciplinary learning and research. Its focus on works that transformed their disciplines and its rigorous approach, drawing on the world's leading experts and educational institutions, opens up a world-class education to anyone.'

Andreas Schleicher
Director for Education and Skills, Organisation for Economic
Co-operation and Development

'Macat is taking on some of the major challenges in university education … They have drawn together a strong team of active academics who are producing teaching materials that are novel in the breadth of their approach.'

Prof Lord Broers,
former Vice-Chancellor of the University of Cambridge

'The Macat vision is exceptionally exciting. It focuses upon new modes of learning which analyse and explain seminal texts which have profoundly influenced world thinking and so social and economic development. It promotes the kind of critical thinking which is essential for any society and economy.
This is the learning of the future.'

Rt Hon Charles Clarke, former UK Secretary of State for Education

'The Macat analyses provide immediate access to the critical conversation surrounding the books that have shaped their respective discipline, which will make them an invaluable resource to all of those, students and teachers, working in the field.'

Professor William Tronzo, University of California at San Diego

WAYS IN TO THE TEXT

KEY POINTS

- Born in 1938, Jonathan Riley-Smith is one of the most important historians of the Crusades* (a series of military invasions of the Middle East by European armies in the medieval period,* conducted with the declared aim of reclaiming Christian holy sites from the Muslim inhabitants).

- *The First Crusade and the Idea of Crusading* analyses how the idea of a "Crusade" was first proposed and how that concept evolved during and following the First Crusade* of 1096–99, both by the people who took part and those who chronicled its success afterward.

- *The First Crusade* is a landmark text that presents Riley-Smith's revisionist* argument that the Crusaders were motivated not by power, greed, or fanaticism, but, rather, by genuine religious faith and the environment of their times ("revisionist" history challenges and revises the consensus with regard to a historical subject).

Who Is Jonathan Riley-Smith?

The author of *The First Crusade and the Idea of Crusading* (1986), Jonathan Riley-Smith, was born in 1938 into a prosperous family, beginning his education at the elite Eton College and going on to

Trinity College, Cambridge. A professor and historian of the Crusades for over 50 years, he began his academic career in 1964 as assistant lecturer in the department of medieval history at the University of St. Andrews in Scotland. As his career progressed, he joined Cambridge University and the University of London, moving back to Cambridge in 1994 to become the Dixie Professor of Ecclesiastical History (the history of the church) in the faculties of history and divinity. He was the chair of the faculty of history in Cambridge from 1997 to 2002.

Married to Louise Riley-Smith, an accomplished portrait artist, he is now a fellow of Emmanuel College, Cambridge. Riley-Smith is regarded as the greatest living historian of the Crusades, and is certainly the most important since Steven Runciman,* the British historian whose three-volume *A History of the Crusades* (1951–54) was seen as the final word on the era until some of its arguments were challenged over two decades later in Riley-Smith's first book, *What Were the Crusades?* (1977).

What Does *The First Crusade and the Idea of Crusading* Say?

The First Crusade is an examination of the development of the concept of Crusading, from the initial call to arms by the head of the European branch of Christianity Pope Urban II* in 1095, to the gathering of armies and pilgrims throughout Europe, and the aftermath of the successful First Crusade, when Western European chroniclers began writing the first histories of the campaign, even as more armies were sent eastwards. Those early writers took the rough ideas of Crusading, as developed during the campaigns by the Crusaders themselves, and polished them into more developed and academic arguments. These would be used as canon law (Church law) by Church leaders for centuries to come.

Riley-Smith looks at how Pope Urban II, the spiritual leader of what was officially a nonviolent religion, framed the arguments to justify making war and killing in the name of Jesus Christ. He also examines how the Pope's call to arms was then taken up and understood by the lay population (people not involved in the institution of the Church) of Christian Europe, whose knowledge of Church and canon law would have been small in comparison.

To carry out this task, Riley-Smith not only uses the official records and chronicles of the First Crusade, the public documents, but also a number of new or previously underused materials, such as local church records. Furthermore, he analyses the data electronically, using early spreadsheet technology to cross-reference family and feudal connections between hundreds of participants in the Crusades, combining ancient and modern in a volume widely considered the best on the subject.

The book is not by any means a complete history of the Crusades, or even the First Crusade, but an exploration of how an idea developed through one of the most desperate and dangerous mass movements in history. Readers will learn that the immediate cause of the First Crusade was to come to the aid of hard-pressed Eastern Christians in the Byzantine Empire* (the successor state to the Roman Empire in southeastern Europe and Asia Minor), suffering internal rebellions and under continual attack from Islamic kingdoms to the south and east.

The aims of the First Crusade expanded almost immediately to the (wildly) optimistic goal of liberating the city of Jerusalem from the Islamic Arab forces then holding it. Although Jerusalem had been in the hands of various Arabic dynasties for well over four centuries by this point, it had originally been a Christian city of the old Roman Empire, and later the Byzantine Empire. The European crusaders, marching to the call of the Pope, aimed to liberate the city in the same manner they had recently reclaimed nearer lands from the Byzantines.

The Pope offered the Crusade as a means to salvation—forgiveness for sins, allowing passage to heaven. This was a further incentive to the knights who had spent most of their lives in conflict in their home countries and were now able to use their skills at warfare for what they believed to be a noble cause. Riley-Smith's research shows that, far from being a gold-hungry mob, eager for blood in the lands of the Middle East,* the Europeans who went on the First Crusade were largely professional soldiers and leaders. Rather than seeking riches, they were actually forced to sell almost everything they owned to pay their passage to the other side of the known world.

Why Does *The First Crusade and the Idea of Crusading* Matter?

The First Crusade matters, in short, because it argues against the consensus views of the Crusades held by writers and historians since the start of the Reformation* (the series of protests against the Catholic* church that led to the founding of the Protestant* branch of Christianity in the early 1500s). According to these views, the campaigns' participants were either fanatics motivated by superstition, sadists who relished the idea of killing those of another faith, or most popularly, opportunists who saw the declaration of war in the East as an easy chance to get rich.

While Riley-Smith does not reject the idea that there were some participants in the First Crusade who were so motivated (as there would be in any project of this nature involving tens of thousands of people), he claims that those who embarked on the Crusade in 1095–96 took part in what he describes as a "penitential war" (combat as a means of penitence) mainly for selfless reasons, to atone for their sins.

The First Crusade is a key work for gaining a deeper understanding of the origins and development of one of the most important events of world history. It is also a lesson in the notion that unquestioned ideas are not to be trusted and that thorough research will often allow us a means to successfully question them.

Riley-Smith's work on the Crusades has been perhaps the most influential example of revisionist history of the late twentieth and early twenty-first century. During his early career in the 1960s he began studying the Crusade's knightly orders*—institutions made up of men observing the obligations of both the military and monastery—using pioneering and painstaking research techniques. These studies led him to take a new look at the motivations of the men and women who decided to give up their lives at home and travel to the Holy Land during the medieval period. His arguments that the Crusades were undertaken for selfless motives were completely new, flying in the face of the criticisms of the Crusades dating as far back as the sixteenth century.

SECTION 1
INFLUENCES

MODULE 1
THE AUTHOR AND THE
HISTORICAL CONTEXT

KEY POINTS

- *The First Crusade and the Idea of Crusading* was the third of a series of books in which Jonathan Riley-Smith changed the modern understanding of the Crusades.*

- By the time of the book's publication in 1986, Professor Riley-Smith had been studying the Crusades and the Crusading Orders* (institutions resembling both the monastery and the military) for well over two decades.

- While some of Riley-Smith's other works have drawn links between the Crusades and more modern eras, *The First Crusade and the Idea of Crusading* is limited to understanding the Crusaders* strictly within their own time frame.

Why Read This Text?

Through the publication of three key works—*What Were the Crusades?* (1977), *The Crusades: Idea and Reality 1095–1274* (1981) cowritten with his wife Louise Riley-Smith, and *The First Crusade and the Idea of Crusading* (1986)—Jonathan Riley-Smith questioned what we know about the Crusades, permanently changing the understanding of that key period for a generation of scholars. A fourth book, *The First Crusaders, 1095–1131,* was published in 1997.

Before he wrote those books, modern Crusader studies were based on the work of the eminent British historian Steven Runciman,* who had ended his own three-volume study of the Crusades by condemning them as a "long act of intolerance in the name of God."[1]

> **❝** Over the last thirty years or so, a generation of British scholars led by figures like Giles Constable and the British doyen of crusade studies, Jonathan Riley-Smith, has transformed perceptions of the nature of Crusading. **❞**
>
> Eamon Duffy, *New York Review of Books*

Riley-Smith challenged this view, arguing that the Crusades were a "genuinely devotional activity."[2] He wrote that while the Crusaders' methods may be open to criticism, particularly from a modern point of view, they were acceptable within their own context.

The First Crusade is a work of revisionist* history, questioning and changing our understanding of the history it covers. It also confirms Riley-Smith's status as a historians' historian; in the book, he goes into some detail on his methods of research and analysis, offering much to the undergraduate student seeking to get to grips with the basics of historiography* (the study of how history is written) and also to those outside academia, where serious research and criticism is required.

At the time Riley-Smith was writing the book, events were drawing the attention of the West to the Islamic world and the history of the Crusades. But even he could not have foreseen how important the text would become nearly three decades later, when events such as the terrorist attacks on the United States of September 11, 2001 (9/11*), the Iraq War* of 2003–11, and the Syrian Civil War* that began in 2001, have led to continued reexaminations of the relevance of the Crusades to the twenty-first century.

Author's Life

Jonathan Riley-Smith was born in 1938. As a boy, he attended the elite Eton College, a private secondary school in England attended recently by male members of the British royal family. Like most men his age, his earliest memories would have been dominated by the events of World War II* (1939–45) and its immediate aftermath.

He obtained a bachelor's degree from Trinity College, Cambridge, in 1960, followed by a master's and then a PhD in 1964. From that year until 1972, he was a lecturer of medieval history at the University of St. Andrews, Scotland. He then returned to Cambridge, where he took up a similar role at the university's School of Medieval History. His work was focused not so much on the theory of Crusading, but on the Crusading orders* established in the Levant* (roughly present-day Syria, Lebanon, Israel, Palestine, and Egypt) following the success of the First Crusade.* Devout in their religious practice, these orders observed austere lifestyles. It was from these studies that Riley-Smith developed his interest in the motivations and concepts of Crusading.

As a fellow of Queen's College, Cambridge, Riley-Smith published his first major work of revisionist Crusading history, *What Were the Crusades?*, in 1977. The following year, he moved to Royal Holloway, a college of the University of London, where he remained until 1994. He was a founding member in 1980 of the Society for the Study of the Crusades and the Latin East, and served as its president from 1987 to 1995; he was a professor of ecclesiastical history at Emmanuel College, Cambridge, from 1994 to 2005.[3]

David Abulafia, professor of Mediterranean history at Cambridge University, wrote that "Jonathan Riley-Smith has had a greater impact on the study of the Crusades than any living scholar, and his command of every aspect of Crusading, from the identity of participants to the history of the Latin kingdom of Jerusalem, is exceptional."[4]

Author's Background

Later, Riley-Smith began to shift his area of study from the military orders of the Crusader states* (Catholic-governed principalities founded during and after the First Crusade of 1096–99) to the theory of Crusading. This shift occurred in the context of the Crusades becoming increasingly relevant to modern politics and international relations—which was not the case when Runciman wrote his history

20 years earlier. The late 1960s and 1970s saw a dramatic rise in conflicts within the Middle East,* with terrorist incidents spilling over into Europe and America.

Most of these conflicts revolved around the status of the state of Israel, which had been established, in the face of intense opposition from the surrounding Arab states, in the very area where the medieval Crusader Kingdom of Jerusalem was located. It was not hard for some political leaders and analysts to draw a connection between the continuing support for Israel by Western countries, especially the United States, and the Western-backed Crusader states of the medieval period.*

The First Crusade can be seen as an attempt to analyze the motivations of the Crusaders, not within the context of the twentieth century, or even the colonial* period prior to that, but within their own place and time. The work also disconnects its analysis from the damaging interpretations that can arise from making such connections.

Riley-Smith has commented on the similarities and differences between the Crusades and events of the modern period, right up to the War on Terror,* (the ongoing US-led fight against Islamic terrorists). His work in *The First Crusade,* however, is an attempt to consider the events and ideas of the Crusaders and their religious and non-Church leaders strictly within their own environment and, as much as possible, in their own words.

NOTES

1   Thomas F. Madden, *The New Concise History of the Crusades* (Baltimore: Rowman and Littlefield, 2005), 216.

2   Kelly Boyd, ed., *Encyclopedia of Historians and Historical Writing, Volume 1* (London: Routledge, 1999), 268.

3   Jonathan Riley-Smith, "The Gifford Lectures," accessed December 12, 2015, http://www.giffordlectures.org/lecturers/jonathan-riley-smith.

4   David Abulafia, quoted by Bloomsbury Publishing, accessed January 6, 2015, http://www.bloomsbury.com/uk/the-crusades-a-history-9781472514820/#sthash.TcmJB9fA.dpuf.

MODULE 2
ACADEMIC CONTEXT

KEY POINTS

- For more than four centuries, the Crusades* were widely understood as a movement motivated mainly by religious fanaticism and the chance to loot treasure from the Holy Land.

- Jonathan Riley-Smith concluded that Crusaders* were motivated by religious devotion and the desire to do penance* (actions performed to atone for sin according to Roman Catholic* doctrine); he found that almost no other modern historian had examined the Crusades in this way.

- Riley-Smith became interested in the subject while studying the Christian liberation* movements of the 1970s in Latin America; like the Roman Catholic Church of the Middle Ages,* these movements developed the idea of the justified use of violence.

The Work in its Context

Jonathan Riley-Smith's *The First Crusade and the Idea of Crusading* (1986) was published at a time when the motives of the Crusades were still largely viewed as almost entirely materialistic* (undertaken for the seizure of land and treasure from the rich Holy Land) and the results as destructive. This was not a new idea. In his protest against the granting of indulgences (the process by which people could have their divine punishment for sins lessened or pardoned by a payment) by the Roman Catholic* Church, the German theologian Martin Luther,* the founder of the Protestant* branch of Christianity, had criticized the Crusaders. Writing in the 1500s, he said they had blindly followed outdated superstition and mindless Catholic

> 66 Scholars have been turning away from the idea that the majority of Crusaders were materialistic in motivation. The image of the landless younger son riding off in search of land and wealth has been replaced by a more complex picture of nobles and knights—very little is known about the peasants—making sacrifices which affected not only themselves but also their families. 99

Jonathan Riley-Smith, *What Were the Crusades?* Preface to the Second Edition

fanaticism by seeking to cancel out their past sins by committing acts—Crusading—that had no bearing on their spiritual well-being.

These criticisms were expanded by eighteenth-century writers like the French philosopher Voltaire* and the English historian Edward Gibbon.* Both supported secularism* (the removal of the Church's influence over non-Church affairs, like government and education) and were open critics of Christianity. As a result, they took the Protestant distaste for the Crusades to a new level and claimed that the wars in the Levant* were motivated by bloodlust and greed. In his work *The History of Decline and Fall of the Roman Empire*, Gibbon wrote that the Crusades were born of a "savage fanaticism."[1]

During the European Age of Imperialism,* the period starting in the 1870s when European countries amassed huge global empires, the Crusading spirit was often mentioned. It was used both by those who supported the building of these empires for religious or material reasons, and by those who cautioned against what they saw as the madness of dominating peoples of other nations. Early twentieth-century Crusade histories were often little more than comparative studies of the methods of colonialism,* in which the Crusader states* formed after the First Crusade* were held to be early colonies in the same mold as those of the nineteenth- and twentieth-century British and French Empires.

In this context, in attempting to restore the reputation of the Crusaders, Riley-Smith's work was groundbreaking because it flew in the face of more than four centuries of criticism.

Overview of the Field

The most recent notable example of such criticism came from Steven Runciman* who, like Riley-Smith, had attended Trinity College, Cambridge. Runciman's three-volume *A History of the Crusade*s (published between 1951 and 1954) had been openly critical of the Crusades as a barbarous venture, similar to the Germanic invasions that brought down the western Roman Empire* in the fifth century C.E.

Runciman's clear sympathy for Byzantine* sources had not marred the achievement of his work on the Crusades. His three volumes were praised not only for the wealth of information and insight that they provided for students and general readers alike, but also for his highly readable writing style that led to a degree of popularity not often seen in medieval history. The historian Thomas F. Madden* says that Runciman is largely responsible for the current popular image of the Crusades, and his work remains on the reading lists of most universities to this day.

Madden claims that Runciman was influenced by the twentieth-century academic trend toward Marxism,* an approach to the analysis of society and history that strongly rejects wars fought to expand religious or state power and, indeed, colonialism* in any form—of which the Crusades were by now seen as an example.

According to Marxist "materialist" analysis, economic (material) matters, notably the struggle between social classes, are the principle drivers of history. Riley-Smith's own opinion is not so much that Marxist writers were responsible for this materialistic view of the Crusades; rather, he felt that most modern "liberal economic historians

… in the 1920s and 1930s began writing of the Crusades, stripped of their ethic, in social and economic terms."[2] ("Liberal" here refers to an approach to the understanding of economic activity according to which the individual, rather than the state, is the most important actor).

Without this vital ingredient of "ethic" (the Crusaders' deep moral and religious motivation), the Crusades could only be seen as a "long act of intolerance against God," which is the way Runciman summed up the Crusades in the closing volume of his history.

Academic Influences

Although Riley-Smith would have been aware of these different currents of opinion, his interest in the motivations of the Crusaders came from an unlikely source: his study of Christian liberation movements in Latin America during the 1970s.[3] The writings of these armed Christian groups influenced him to attempt to write a history of the Christian theology of force (that is, the approval of the use of violence within the law of the Roman Catholic* Church). The huge nature of this project eventually led Riley-Smith to have second thoughts about committing to it fully, but not before he came up with a theory about the First Crusade, no doubt drawing on his own academic past as a student of the Crusader orders* of the period. He came to the conclusion that the First Crusade was the foremost event in which Christian theories of war were finally made official and put into practice.

Pope Urban II* had drawn on writers like the influential fifth-century religious thinker Augustine of Hippo* for the legal basis of his appeal for the faithful to join the First Crusade in 1095. But the theories of how violence could form a part of the almost completely nonviolent rules of Christianity were still just being considered at that stage. It would take the successful completion of the First Crusade in 1099 before those ideas of a "just war" were fully developed.

Finding that only a single writer, the French historian Jean Barthélémy Richard, had explored similar ideas (and then only in the preface to a book of translated texts), Riley-Smith decided to start studying the *idea* of Crusading. He wanted to prove, as he put it, that the materialist, Marxist, and liberal economic explanations of the Crusades were wrong, and built on insecure foundations.[4]

NOTES

1   Jonathan Phillips, "The Call of the Crusades," *History Today* 59, no. 11, (2009), accessed January 6 2016, http://www.historytoday.com/jonathan-phillips/call-crusades.

2   Jonathan Riley-Smith, *The First Crusade and the Idea of Crusading,* 2nd ed. (London: Continuum, 2009), 6.

3   Riley-Smith, *The First Crusade*, 3.

4   Riley-Smith, *The First Crusade*, 4–7.

MODULE 3
THE PROBLEM

KEY POINTS

- *The First Crusade* is solely concerned with understanding the ideas of those who took part in the Crusades.*

- In this light, Jonathan Riley-Smith was determined that the book would not seek to judge the participants.

- Although his conclusions and arguments were criticized by many, he also helped found a new school of revisionist* historians of the Crusades.

Core Question

While Jonathan Riley-Smith's original intention was to write a sweeping history of the Christian theory of war, this is not much in evidence in *The First Crusade and the Idea of Crusading*. Instead, the book focuses entirely on the events from the initial organization of the First Crusade* in 1095 to the appearance of the first written histories of the campaign in the following decades. The personalities and incidents under discussion relate only to the First Crusade and its immediate aftermath. At the heart of the book is the search for an answer to the question of how Western Christians, whose church and leader preached nonviolence, came to launch and then justify a religiously motivated military campaign across two continents.

Riley-Smith's sole aim is to examine how the concept of an armed pilgrimage to the Holy Land was proposed and developed, before the idea was eventually refined and polished into a theological concept for the public by three monastic writers: Robert the Monk,* Guibert of Nogent,* and Baldric of Borgueil.* Each of these monk historians, writing separately but drawing on a single original text—the *Gesta*

> **❝ Thus far the gap between historical understanding and popular perception remains great. ❞**
>
> Thomas F. Madden, *The New Concise History of the Crusades*

Francorum* (Deeds of the Franks*), written during or just after the First Crusade—documented the medieval concept of the Crusades.

Seeking to understand the motives of Christian religious warriors was very much against the fashion in 1970s Europe and the United States. Britain was affected by the "Troubles"* in Northern Ireland, where Roman Catholic* and Protestant* groups were in violent conflict, and a sympathetic portrayal of war for religious reasons was positively unwelcome. In other parts of Europe, both East and West, religious wars had long fallen off the radar. The belief systems of the day were communism* (the state ideology of the Soviet Union) and free market capitalism* (the dominant social and political philosophy of the West, notably the United States and Britain). It would be almost another decade before the break-up of the state of Yugoslavia* and the conflict between the Christian and Muslim people of the "new" states of Serbia and Bosnia would alert the world to the continued existence of seemingly ancient, but still dangerous, divisions.

Though Middle Eastern wars occasionally spilled over into Europe and even affected the United States—in such events as the terrorist attack on the 1972 Munich Olympics* and the Iranian hostage crisis* of 1979—they were not popularly considered of great significance. From his own comments, it would appear that Riley-Smith's motivation in writing about the First Crusade and its ideologies was intellectual curiosity rather than a need to address a current problem.[1]

The Participants

During this period one of Riley-Smith's fellow scholars, the Marxist* historian Geoffrey Barraclough,* turned to the Crusades in order to understand the present, publishing a series of books on medieval Europe as viewed through his own ideological and modernist standpoint, including *The Mediaeval Empire: Idea and Reality* (1950) and *The Christian World: A Social and Cultural History of Christianity* (1981). Like Steven Runciman,* he denounced the Crusades as what he called "that first age of European colonialism"* and had no problem applying terms like "brutal," "rapacious," and "predatory" to events that he stated were the first step on a long violent road toward the extreme right-wing nationalism of Nazi* Germany.[2]

Barraclough's work can be seen as the opposite of what Riley-Smith was attempting to do in *The First Crusade*—to examine the events and people of the era within their own circumstances and the spirit of the times, without the prejudices of later events and systems of morality. Writing in the post-World War II* period of the twentieth century (a period of reconstruction and reconciliation following the defeat of the genocidal regime of Nazi Germany in Europe in 1945), Barraclough made no bones about the fact that he was viewing the Crusades through reality as he saw it. But Riley-Smith, on the other hand, was equally unapologetic in his intention to be as sympathetic to the Crusaders as he could. He aimed to understand how it was that so many men and women volunteered to leave behind family and friends and embark on a journey that they knew would likely involve severe hardship, poverty, and eventual death in a strange land.

The Contemporary Debate

Riley-Smith was an established and successful academic when *The First Crusade* was published in 1986. His earlier works in a similar vein had already earned him a reputation within academic circles as a revisionist historian of some standing. But *The First Crusade* and its follow-up *The First Crusaders, 1095–1131*, published in 1997 on the thousand-year anniversary of the first major battles of the Crusade, cemented his position as the leading living historian of the Crusades (and perhaps the most widely cited).

Though he has no shortage of admirers, Riley-Smith engages with those who disagree with his findings, some of which are controversial. For example, in the introduction to the 2009 edition of *The First Crusade,* he admits the accuracy of Susanna Throop's criticisms of his claim that the anti-Jewish feelings among Roman Catholics* in Western Europe declined after the pogroms that marked the start of the First Crusade.

Riley-Smith's findings have had a major influence on modern scholars of the Crusades, notably the US historian Thomas F. Madden* and the British historians Jonathan Phillips* and Christopher Tyerman.* Like Riley-Smith, they have attempted, when possible, to represent the historical figures and events of the Crusades as products of their own place and time, albeit with distinct modern echoes. All of these writers have avoided the easy condemnations and judgmental attitudes that were a hallmark of past historians like Runciman and Barraclough.

NOTES

1   Jonathan Riley-Smith, *The First Crusade and the Idea of Crusading,* 2nd ed. (London: Continuum, 2009), 1–3.

2   Geoffrey Barraclough, "Deus le Volt?" *New York Review of Books,* May 21 1970, accessed January 6, 2016, http://www.nybooks.com/articles/1970/05/21/deus-le-volt/.

MODULE 4
THE AUTHOR'S CONTRIBUTION

KEY POINTS

- In *The First Crusade*, Riley-Smith asserts that the concept of how a war could be fought in the name of Christianity developed over at least four distinct stages.

- The author turned to previously unexamined original sources, especially archives of Church manuscripts; he also pioneered the use of computer spreadsheets to organize and compare the data.

- His use of new medieval sources and modern computer technology helped changed the methods used by historians working on the period.

Author's Aims

Jonathan Riley-Smith's main aim in writing *The First Crusade and the Idea of Crusading* was to develop his claim that when Pope Urban II* proclaimed the First Crusade* in 1095 its purpose was not clear and was only clarified in the heat and grind of the campaign itself. From the Crusaders'* point of view, it was a defensive and selfless war in which Christian warriors fought in order to do penance to God for their sins. This became the official story when the main body of survivors returned home and the record keepers of various monasteries were able to write down their accounts of what had happened.

So the idea and purpose of Crusading was not the will or work of just one man, body, or institution but an ongoing process that lasted for at least a decade. Riley-Smith's approach was unique: no other historian had previously focused on the reasons for fighting. Most general histories of the Crusade used only extracts of the

> **❝**Jonathan Riley-Smith ... guided me through university life as an undergraduate and postgraduate, teaching me the principles of historical research and the value of critical analysis... **❞**
>
> Thomas Asbridge, *The First Crusade: A New History*

Pope's speech, of which there are at least five different versions, some of them certainly written by people who did not hear the Pope speak in person.

Riley-Smith broke the First Crusade down into sections. First came Urban's call to arms at the Council of Clermont* (a Church council convened in 1095). This was followed by the Pope's tour around Frankish* towns (towns in Frankia—France; Crusaders themselves are often known as "Franks"). Then came three waves of actual Crusading bodies who travelled to the East. Finally came the work of the latter historians like the French monk Guibert of Nogent.*

By breaking the Crusades down in this manner, like a forensic scientist investigating a crime, Riley-Smith was able to trace how the relatively simple yet confused appeals that Urban made became a more sophisticated rationale for a "just war." Notably, this version of events lacked the more negative motivations (greed and the desire to plunder, as well as religious fanaticism) that earlier historians had given it.

Approach
Riley-Smith's approach to answering the question of how the idea of Christian holy war developed was unique in two ways.

First, during the late 1980s, he had begun using a form of spreadsheet technology to accumulate details of individual Crusaders and their families and to cross-reference them. In this way, he was able to identify points of contact between certain individuals and even construct family trees with unprecedented efficiency. While today such digitalized mapping and cross-referencing might seem standard practice, it must be remembered that computer technology for private and even academic purposes was still in its infancy during the period he was writing. Historians tend not to be too quick to embrace new technology, so Riley-Smith's willingness to master a new method meant that his history gained an extra dimension that was lacking in other work on the same topic.

Second, for the research materials to feed into the computer, Riley-Smith did not simply rely on well-known sources that had been used many times, like the early twelfth-century *Gesta Francorum** and other chronicles. Instead, he looked for previously unexamined material. This search led him to the discovery of piles of handwritten Church documents (known as cartularies*): collections of title deeds, wills, and loans, sometimes with other information, which provided a record of how families and individuals prepared to embark on a quest as challenging as the Crusade to the Holy Land.

These documents were to be found in cathedrals and monasteries all over France, Germany, and Britain, and through them Riley-Smith was able to identify the biographical details of at least two hundred individuals who had embarked on the First Crusade, never having been previously mentioned in any historical work.[1] Even more tantalizingly, many of these collections of documents, particularly those from Burgundy and other regions of France, included written accounts of how and why the men organizing their affairs had decided to go on Crusade.

Contribution in Context

While Riley-Smith credits the English historian Giles Constable* with first drawing attention to the information in medieval cartularies,* he has also pointed out that the records remain largely unexamined to this day, even after his own considerable efforts to sift through the material. Fifteen years after the publication of *The First Crusade*, Riley-Smith wrote that there are at least 1,500 collections of documents relating to the Crusading era that have been printed by archivists, not to mention thousands of others in religious communities all over the continent. He made this estimate on the basis that he had himself read through about half that number, almost all from England and France. But he had merely glimpsed a fraction of what was available in Spain, Italy, and Germany.[2] Certainly his own contributions toward placing these invaluable historical accounts in the public domain have been considerable.

His blending of the ancient with the modern, running thousand-year-old Church documents through a computer and looking for connections, established a new model that historians, even those well advanced in their careers, could follow. With this new approach, Riley-Smith and the historians who succeeded him, such as John France,* were able to give precise statistics of the age, wealth, and social connections of the participants in the Crusades. These historians also led the way for such studies to be expanded into other areas beyond the medieval period.*

NOTES

1 Jonathan Riley-Smith, introduction to *The First Crusade: Origins and Impact*, ed. Jonathan Phillips (Manchester: Manchester University Press, 1997), 3.

2 Riley-Smith, intro to *The First Crusade: Origins and Impact*, 3.

SECTION 2
IDEAS

MODULE 5
MAIN IDEAS

KEY POINTS

- The book starts by discussing the several competing definitions of a "Crusade"—is a Crusade any military campaign approved by the Roman Catholic* pope, or only those campaigns that seek to capture the holy city of Jerusalem?

- Riley-Smith discusses how the hardships and successes of the First Crusade* led the Church to develop and make official the idea of Crusading.

- *The First Crusade* is presented in six chapters, each devoted to a specific phase of the Crusade, with an introduction and conclusion bookending the volume.

Key Themes

The First Crusade and the Idea of Crusading in many ways follows and expands on the themes that Jonathan Riley-Smith had already begun to explore in his 1977 book *What Were the Crusades?* In *The Crusades* (1965), the German Crusade historian Hans Eberhard Mayer* had already highlighted the "lack of any agreed, precise definition" of what a Crusade actually was. This was the case despite the long-running public interest in the period throughout the Western world.[1] In what way, he and others asked, were the Crusades different from the near-contemporary Reconquista* of Spain, in which Roman Catholic forces drove out the Muslim Arabs, for example?

At the time he published his earlier book *What Were the Crusades?* Riley-Smith argued that any military campaign that was approved by the pope qualified as a Crusade. This directly contradicted Mayer's position that conquering Jerusalem had to be the central goal of

> ❝ The starting point for any study of the Crusades must be what the Church, their justifier and authorizer, thought of them. ❞
>
> Jonathan Riley-Smith, *What Were the Crusades?* Preface to the Second Edition

anything termed a Crusade, and it also significantly widened the time period of the Crusading era, beyond the medieval and into the early-modern period (that is, up to the end of the eighteenth century). Those who followed Riley-Smith's school of thought in this matter were labelled "pluralists"* among Crusade scholars, as they opened the discipline to a plurality (a variety) of new eras and historical events.[2]

A softening of Riley-Smith's stance on the issue is visible in *The First Crusade*, however. As the narrative goes on and he recounts the thought processes of the mystics, Church officials, and nobles on the campaign, and the reverence in which they held Jerusalem (a city holy to Christians, Muslims, and Jews), it becomes clear that the idea of crusading and of holy war itself would not have been possible without the holy city as its goal. It had, he states, a huge hold on the imaginations of the men involved.

Exploring the Ideas

The First Crusade has a simple central theme: the concept of Christian holy war was put together and made official with the success of the First Crusade. According to this concept, when men fight a holy war, God will not only allow them to do violence but, as a reward, will actually forgive them for their past sins. Riley-Smith is clear that without the success of the First Crusade, more conservative parts of the Church hierarchy would have taken the lead and made sure that no other such campaign in God's name was attempted again. It was the success of the First Crusade and the sacrifices that its devout army of pilgrims made that transformed it into something so special that it could be termed a "holy" war.

Riley-Smith goes into the details of these sacrifices and hardships, using firsthand accounts of those who took part. He relates how Crusaders who were nobles often sold or mortgaged their lands, in many cases making themselves landless in the process and without the means to provide for themselves and their families should they return alive. He recounts the lack of food (sometimes resulting in death from starvation), the attacks from locals even before the Crusaders had left Christian Europe, and the huge disadvantage that the Crusader army found itself in when faced by the more advanced Islamic states.

Yet, set against the hardship, illness, and constant violence are many stories of miracles. These included the Crusaders' military victories at Doryleum* (a settlement in what is today northwest Turkey), Antioch* (a city in southern Turkey), and Jerusalem,* which any military specialist would argue were so unlikely as to be unthinkable. There were also countless natural phenomena witnessed by the Crusaders across the Middle East that they interpreted as divine signs: comets, earthquakes, auroras (a natural phenomenon of reddish or greenish lights in the sky), and even an eclipse. These all added to the notion, Riley-Smith says, that the Crusaders were involved in a supernatural undertaking.[3]

Thus, while Pope Urban II's* appeal had merely been for pious fighting men to travel and aid their fellow Christians and liberate cities, the Crusaders came to believe that they actually *were* the instruments of God's hand. While this might seem laughable by modern standards, as Riley-Smith makes clear in *The First Crusade*, it was a perfectly acceptable idea at the time. It should also be noted that of the eight or so following Crusades directed at the Levant,* none succeeded in even matching the initial successes of the First Crusade as it crossed Anatolia (modern-day Turkey). In fact, for a campaign that even remotely resembled the First Crusade in terms of speed and success over the same ground, one must look back to the lightning campaigns of the ancient Macedonian leader Alexander the Great,* fourteen hundred years earlier.

Language and Expression

The six chapters of *The First Crusade* are really interconnected essays and all can be read separately. The chapters run chronologically, from the sermon Urban gave in 1095 calling for Jerusalem to be retaken and the response of the lay people, to conditions on the march, the ideas of the Crusaders, the Crusade of 1101, and the adjustments made to Christian theology to include the idea of Crusading in the following years.

Although a book of this sort could be complicated and difficult to read, this is by no means the case with the language and extracts from the sources employed by Riley-Smith. The author has done a remarkable job of getting inside the Crusaders' heads and making their thoughts understandable to a modern audience, who feel as if they are actually on the march with the army. Riley-Smith's translations are clear and without any archaic expressions. In consequence, the voices of Crusaders are direct and moving. Here, for example, Pope Urban II states that fighters of pure heart will be automatically forgiven all previous sins:"Whoever for devotion only, not to gain honor or money, goes to Jerusalem to liberate the Church of God can substitute this journey for all penance."[4]

The book represents a considerable technical achievement in bringing so many different voices and ideas together in one volume. And though *The First Crusade* is a more specialized text than a general history, it is a book that can be read and understood by anyone with an interest in the events or the historical period, from first-year undergraduates to newcomers looking to understand just what the Crusades were about.

NOTES

1   Norman Housely, Review of The Invention of the Crusades, by
    Christopher Tyerman, *The International History Review* 21, no. 2
    (1999), 455–7, accessed January 6, 2016, http://www.jstor.org/
    stable/40109013?seq=1#page_scan_tab_contents.

2   Housely, Review of *The Invention of the Crusade.*

3   Jonathan Riley-Smith, *The First Crusade and the Idea of Crusading,* 2nd ed.
    (London: Continuum, 2009), 92.

4   Riley-Smith, *The First Crusade*, 29.

MODULE 6
SECONDARY IDEAS

KEY POINTS

- In coming to the conclusion that the First Crusade* was a devotional war, Riley-Smith dismissed the long-standing theory that the Crusades* had been undertaken for the acquisition of wealth and land in what might be understood as an early example of European colonialism* (the exploitative occupation of foreign territory).

- This materialist* understanding—an interpretation of history founded on economic factors—had been engrained in the collective imagination by popular historical romance books of the early nineteenth century.

- Although nineteenth-century historians in France and Germany had lauded the achievements of the Crusades, Riley-Smith's positive portrayal of the Crusaders* was the reverse of centuries of criticism in the English-speaking world.

Other Ideas

One of the accepted ideas that Jonathan Riley-Smith questions from the outset of *The First Crusade and the Idea of Crusading* is what he termed the "materialist" argument. This was the belief, promoted by various groups over many years, that the Crusades were undertaken to gain wealth and land, rather than for doing penance for one's sins—the reason given at the time by the Crusaders themselves and also by medieval historians. Crusader wealth, or the lack of it, is a theme that runs just below the surface throughout the book. Riley-Smith uses it to strengthen the book's main theme of how the idea of the Crusade as a devotional war (a war fought for deep religious motivations) developed over the period.

> ❝ More recently charters [Church records] have begun to be used as a source of Crusading history by several scholars ... most notably Jonathan Riley Smith. ❞
>
> Giles Constable, *Crusaders and Crusading in the Twelfth Century*

The belief that Crusaders sought wealth stems from one of the many versions of Pope Urban II's* speech calling for the Crusade in 1095—that of the twelfth-century chronicler Robert the Monk.* In it, Urban is alleged to have urged his audience to "Take the road to [Jerusalem], rescue that land and rule over it yourselves, for that land, as the scripture says, floweth with milk and honey".[1] This mention of "milk and honey," despite being written 20 years after the speech was given, has been seized on for many years as evidence that the Pope and the Crusaders had money in mind when they started their armed pilgrimage. This idea was strengthened by the fact that the Crusaders established their own states in the Levant* once the Crusade was ultimately successful.

Exploring the Ideas

Riley-Smith steadily demolishes these arguments throughout *The First Crusade*, making it clear that very few, if any, of the Crusaders and their leaders became wealthy from the campaign. "There is little evidence of them returning rich in anything but relics," he says and, of course, relics (bones of the saints, small pieces of ancient churches and tombs, and so on) could only be donated to the Church.[2] *The First Crusade* contains many examples of the poverty of the Crusaders. When examining the response of the lay people to the Pope's message, Riley-Smith draws attention to the fact that many knights, castellans (the captain of a castle), and magnates (wealthy people) sold off a large proportion of their land in exchange for cash to use for their journey to the Levant. This could range from the small scale (the Frankish* knight Hugh Bochard* sold a house for the equivalent of five dollars and a mule) to the colossal: Bishop Otbert of Liege* stripped his cathedral of valuables to fund his lord, Godfrey of Bouillon's,* journey; and Robert of Normandy,* son of William the Conqueror,* mortgaged the entire Duchy of Normandy to his brother, King William II of England, for the gigantic sum of 10,000 silver marks, forcing him to sharply hike English taxes in order to raise the money.[3]

Riley-Smith makes it clear that "a commitment to Crusade ... involved heavy expenses and real financial sacrifices," and that leaving one's self open to such financial embarrassment in the remote hope of winning some eastern fiefdom was, simply, a "stupid gamble."[4] Also, as Robert's case makes plain, there was clearly a large group of people willing to make personal sacrifices to allow others to go on Crusade while they stayed at home. What did they have to gain?

The first of Urban's two goals for the Crusade (the second being to claim Jerusalem) was the extension of aid to Eastern Christians following an appeal for assistance from the Byzantine* emperor Alexius I Comnenus,* who was beset by internal and external threats. As a result, Urban would have expected that any conquests be carried out in the name of the Byzantine emperor, not the Roman Catholic* Church. It was only in light of squabbling, caused mainly by the culture clash between the rough Franks and the reserved Byzantines, that the Crusaders kept the newly established Crusader states* once the area had been secured. Keeping land was never part of the plan, as shown by the return of nearly the entire Crusading army after the final battles, leaving few fighters behind to garrison the new kingdoms. In any case, whatever loot they had managed to grab during the taking of Jerusalem would most likely have been spent on the return journey home.

Overlooked

While scholars have taken the arguments of *The First Crusade* seriously, on the whole they have failed to enter the mainstream. In the last decade two presidents of the United States, Bill Clinton* and Barack Obama,* have referred to the climax of the First Crusade as an example of fanatical, mindless violence. The presidents completely ignored both the context of the campaign and the necessary insight, as provided by Riley-Smith, for a proper understanding of what the First Crusade involved.

Both Clinton and Obama's condemnation concentrated on the deaths that occurred after the taking of Jerusalem* in 1099, when the city's population was either massacred or imprisoned. Unfortunately, this was typical—as any reading of medieval history will show. Imprisonment, forced conversion, and execution were also practiced regularly by the Islamic forces opposing the Crusaders, which the capture of one French knight, Raynald Porchet,* vividly demonstrates.[5] In fact, the early battles of *The First Crusade* are so full of examples of death and suffering on both sides that the fall of Jerusalem seems unremarkable by the time one reaches it.

Such is Riley-Smith's reputation that his work was mentioned in the press coverage of President Obama's comments.[6] But it is nonetheless significant that 30 years after *The First Crusade's* publication, the book's main ideas have still not changed attitudes or etched themselves into the collective consciousness in even the most informed circles.

NOTES

1   Jonathan Phillips, *Holy Warriors: A Modern History of the Crusades* (London: Bodley Head, 2009), 1.

2   Jonathan Riley-Smith, *The First Crusade and the Idea of Crusading,* 2nd ed. (London: Continuum, 2009), 41.

3   Riley-Smith, *The First Crusade*, 44.

4   Riley-Smith, *The First* Crusade, 47.

5   Riley-Smith, *The First* Crusade, 115.

6   Jay Michaelson, "The Crusades Were Great Actually!", *The Daily Beast*, October 2, 2015, accessed 15 Dec. 2015, http://www.thedailybeast.com/articles/2015/02/10/the-crusades-were-great-actually.html.

MODULE 7
ACHIEVEMENT

KEY POINTS

- *The First Crusade* succeeded in its goal of accurately presenting (as far as possible) the psychology of the participants of the First Crusade* and explaining why they behaved in such an extraordinary manner.

- This success is down to a combination of Riley-Smith's innovative and tireless scholarship, an accessible writing style, and a tight structure.

- While the book's arguments have failed to achieve universal recognition, its strengths have led to it becoming part of the ongoing public debate about current Middle Eastern issues.

Assessing the Argument

In *The First Crusade and the Idea of Crusading,* Jonathan Riley-Smith relies heavily on the insights provided by primary sources. Chief among these are the collections of cartularies,* as well as better-known sources like Pope Urban II's* sermon, the *Gesta Francorum** (an account possibly written during the Crusade itself), and the work of three monastic writers who refined the message of Crusading once the Crusade had come to a close. Apart from some short references in the introduction to a few modern scholars, the text does not cite any modern writers or ideas, making *The First Crusade* as near as possible a complete canvas of Crusading ideas as they existed at the time of the Crusade. In particular, the work is notable for its accumulation of detailed information on the social and family connections of individual Crusaders, an achievement on which Riley-Smith has built his reputation.

> **❝** He concludes that Urban's message at Clermont was conventional but the response was not. **❞**
>
> John Gilchrist, Review of *The First Crusade and the Idea of Crusading*

The First Crusade goes closely through the recorded reactions of the Crusaders to their experiences on the Crusade, from the ordeals of battle to the desperate search for food by unpaid men. The book gauges how each of these challenges affected the mindset of those who survived. It must be remembered that the Crusaders travelled in groups, not as an army under one leader, and the fortunes of each individual Crusader varied greatly, according to his position and the lord under whose banner he marched. Many of the Crusaders traveled as individual pilgrims, relying on their own pocket or skills to feed themselves on the campaign. For those who survived all the way to Jerusalem and won victory, it seemed nothing short of a miracle. Riley-Smith emphasizes how tough conditions were. In 1097–98, while the Crusaders were in the city of Antioch* (in today's Turkey), they had to travel up to 50 miles in search of food.[1] It was no wonder then, he states, that having survived against such odds, the Crusaders truly did begin to believe in the holy cause for which they fought. In other words, God *had* to be on their side.

Achievement in Context

A year after *The First Crusade* was published, Riley-Smith's *The First Crusaders: 1095–1131* (1987) was issued. Although this companion work has been translated into French, Italian, and Polish, it appears that there are no plans to do the same with the earlier book.[2] Indeed *The First Crusade* did not appear in paperback in Riley-Smith's native United Kingdom until 1993, seven years after its hardback publication. This is a pity, since it has limited the book's impact, particularly in non-English-speaking regions.

Riley-Smith has often spoken of the necessity for historians to use non-Western sources (indeed, he is listed by Carole Hillenbrand* as an important supporter of her *The Crusades: Islamic Perspectives* (1999), the most considerable attempt to make Arabic* sources on the Crusades accessible in Western markets).[3] However, no attempt has been made, it seems, to translate his own work into Arabic, the language spoken by the vast majority of people who live in the lands targeted by the First Crusade. It is surely likely that the effort to understand why the Crusaders did what they did is something that the modern inhabitants of the Levant*—the people of Syria, Lebanon, Israel, Palestine, and Egypt—would find of interest. Given the area's recent troubles and the lasting legacy of past conflicts, this would seem a pressing issue.

Limitations

If *The First Crusade* has had a huge impact, it has been felt by those within academia and the media rather than the public—a fact perhaps reinforcing Riley-Smith's status as a historian's historian. Notwithstanding his retirement, his ideas remain part of ongoing public discussions.

Writing in 2015, after President Barack Obama* compared the brutality of the First Crusade with that of ISIS/Daesh,* one critic noted that Riley-Smith's theories about the motivations of the Crusaders was especially popular among modern right-wing commentators; he also noted, however, that the same commentators used the historian's findings selectively in order to suit their own agenda.[4] Other commentators have used the author's arguments to make their own criticism of why the President's views were incorrect; still others relied on Riley-Smith's disciples to provide up-to-the-minute reaction quotes.[5]

These were not debates that Riley-Smith could possibly have foreseen when he wrote *The First Crusade* in the 1980s in preparation for the one-thousandth anniversary of the First Crusade. Apart from the 1979 Iranian Revolution,* in which a religious republic was proclaimed, the largely secular* leaders of states like Syria, Iraq, and Egypt had been in power for decades, and it seemed as if that situation would continue indefinitely. It is a mark of Riley-Smith's scholarship that his ideas have remained solid despite the complete transformation of the geopolitical landscape in the intervening years.

NOTES

1   Jonathan Riley-Smith, *The First Crusade and the Idea of Crusading*, 2nd ed. (London: Continuum, 2009), 66.

2   Profile of Jonathan Riley-Smith, *crusaderstudies*, accessed December 15, 2015, http://www.crusaderstudies.org.uk/resources/historians/profiles/riley_smith/index.html.

3   Jonathan Riley-Smith, introduction to *The First Crusade: Origins and Impact*, ed. Jonathan Phillips (Manchester: Manchester University Press, 1997), 2.

4   Jay Michaelson, "The Crusades Were Great Actually!", *The Daily Beast*, October 2, 2015, accessed 15 Dec. 2015, http://www.thedailybeast.com/articles/2015/02/10/the-crusades-were-great-actually.html.

5   Arit John, "Why the Crusades Still Matter," *Bloomberg Politics*, February 6, 2015, accessed December 15, 2015, http://www.bloomberg.com/politics/articles/2015–02-06/why-the-crusades-still-matter; Andrew Holt, "Crusades Were a Reaction to Militant Islam," *Jacksonville.com*, February 10 2015, accessed 15 December, 2015, http://jacksonville.com/business/columnists/2015–02-10/story/guest-column-crusades-were-reaction-islamic-militarism.

MODULE 8
PLACE IN THE AUTHOR'S WORK

KEY POINTS

- Since the mid-1970s Riley-Smith's work has focused on broadening the information available about the true nature of the Crusades* and why they were undertaken.

- In addition to focusing on the ideology of Crusading, Riley-Smith has also written several works on the knightly orders* created to fight in the Crusades.

- *The First Crusade* is perhaps the most direct example of Riley-Smith's revisionist* arguments on the motivations of the Crusaders.*

Positioning

Having already addressed long-running arguments regarding the ideology of the Crusades in his earlier works *What Were the Crusades?* (1977) and *The Crusades: Idea and Reality* (1981), Jonathan Riley-Smith wrote *The First Crusade and the Idea of Crusading* (1986) in the middle period of his career.

What Were the Crusades? addressed the pluralist* definition of the Crusade that extended the practice beyond the Middle Ages* by including other campaigns of conquest approved by the pope (pluralist scholarship questions the view that the Crusades were a limited number of campaigns directed against Islamic Middle Eastern powers, largely undertaken for the motive of acquiring land and treasure). *The Crusades: Idea and Reality* (1981), cowritten with his wife Louise, translated many of the original sources that would go into making the arguments of *The First Crusade*. Between these two works, Riley-Smith wrote the article "Crusading as an Act of Love" (1980), a key

> **❝ All history is revisionist, a response to what others have written. ❞**
>
> Christopher Tyerman, *The Debate on the Crusades*

work in the debate over how to consider the period historically. Much as he would in *The First Crusade,* Riley-Smith began to answer in that article just why Crusaders answered Pope Urban II's* call to "take up the cross" and travel nearly three thousand miles to liberate Jerusalem.

The First Crusade differs from its companion, *The First Crusaders 1095–1131* (1997), in that the latter work explored events in the decades after the end of the First Crusade.* The second book examined the idea of Crusading as a family, or clan, activity, an idea touched on in *The First Crusade* but not fully fleshed out until later.

Integration

Before *What Were the Crusades?* (1977), Riley-Smith wrote two books on medieval orders of knights: *The Knights of St John in Jerusalem and Cyprus c. 1050–1310* (1967) and *The Feudal Nobility and the Kingdom of Jerusalem, 1174–1277* (1973). Although these works concerned the Crusades, they lacked much of the revisionist quality of his work from the late 1970s on. It was his research into the liberation theology of armed Christian groups in Latin America, undertaken in the 1970s, that can truly be said to have changed the path of Riley-Smith's life. It led him to make the study of medieval Christian violence his life's work for the 40 years since.

That is not to say that he has completely abandoned the study of the knightly orders of the Crusader kingdoms. In the early 1990s, he contributed the essay "The Order of St John of England, 1827–1858" to *The Military Orders: Fighting for Faith and Caring for the Sick* (1994), a collection of 42 papers delivered at the International Conference on Military Orders held in London in 1992. The volume's editor

Malcolm Barber, emeritus professor of medieval history at the University of Reading, has written much on the Crusading orders and the Crusader states*[1] over the same period that Riley-Smith has been exploring the causes and definitions of Crusading. It is interesting to wonder if Riley-Smith's own career would have followed a similar pattern had his study of the Christian liberation* movements of 1970s Latin America not given him fresh insights into the theological justifications of violence. Indeed, Riley-Smith has returned to the topic of the orders every 10 years or so, particularly that of the Knights Hospitallers* (an order founded to provide protection for Christian pilgrims to the Holy Land and care for the sick following the First Crusade), publishing two major works on their history—*Hospitallers: The History of the Knights of the Order of St. John* (1999) and *The Knight Hospitaller in the Levant, c. 1070–1309* (2012).

Out of his whole body of work, the book that perhaps best combines Riley-Smith's interest in the military orders and the definition and idea of Crusading is *The Crusades, Christianity, and Islam* (2008), tracing the many groups that became Crusaders from the first pilgrims of the eleventh century right up to the modern era. The book's cover shows nineteenth-century French volunteers serving in a private militia in North Africa, bedecked in updated Crusader attire and armed with rifles—a striking image reminding us that the idea of Crusading did not die out with the passing of the medieval period.*

Significance

The First Crusade could be considered the most important of Riley-Smith's works, as it was the first in which he made use of archival material in the form of medieval Church documents. It could also be seen as expanding on the theme of Crusading as an act of love that he expressed in the 1980 article that has been cited by the historian Thomas F. Madden* as key to the modern historical debate on the Crusades.[2]

In addition to these breakthroughs, there is also the fact that the arguments of *The First Crusade* have had a real-world impact in the years since the terror attacks of 9/11,* the subsequent War on Terror,* the Arab Spring* (the popular uprisings that swept North Africa and much of the Middle East from 2010) and the rise of ISIS/Daesh.* In the Western world there has been much debate over the legacy and meaning of the Crusades in the twenty-first century (helped by the habit of terrorist organizations such as ISIS and al Qaeda of referring to all Westerners as "Crusaders"). Riley-Smith has already provided a modern explanation of what the Crusades meant and has built upon those arguments ever since. As a result, his work has a significance and impact that few other historians have enjoyed. While not the most popular of his works, *The First Crusade* is perhaps the one that will have the most influence over time.

NOTES

1 For an introduction to his work see Malcolm Barber, *The Crusader States* (New Haven: Yale University Press, 2012).

2 Jonathan Riley-Smith, "Crusading as an Act of Love," *History* 65 (1980), 177–92, in *The Crusades: The Essential Readings*, ed. Thomas F. Madden, (Oxford: Blackwell, 2002).

SECTION 3
IMPACT

MODULE 9
THE FIRST RESPONSES

KEY POINTS

- The main criticisms of *The First Crusade* focused not on what might be thought the more obvious points—such as the idea of the Crusade* as a devotional war— but on the debate over what actions could actually be termed a "Crusade."

- Although Riley-Smith is seen as one of the leading historians of the Crusades, he and other scholars continue arguing about various features of that historical period.

- No modern counterpart of Riley-Smith has emerged to argue for the "traditionalist"* school of the Crusades.

Criticism

Writing for the *American Historical Review*, the historian James A. Brundage called Jonathan Riley-Smith's interpretation of events in *The First Crusade and the Idea of Crusading* "provocative"—but he noted that the author's scholarship was "impeccable" and that all his arguments were supported by numerous contemporary documents.[1] Elsewhere, he wrote that Riley-Smith and "others had made a splendid beginning at unravelling the ways in which the process of Crusade recruiting worked," while echoing Riley-Smith in making it clear that there was a lot more to do in the area.[2]

Riley-Smith suggested that violence against European Jews in "vengeance" for their supposed collective responsibility for the crucifixion of Christ peaked with the coming of the First Crusade.* The historian Susanna Throop* argued against that; she agreed with Riley-Smith that the Church's preaching for the First Crusade provoked

> **❝ An excellent starting point is still S. Runciman ... but this should now be complemented by the more recent works of J. S. C. Riley-Smith. ❞**
>
> Carole Hillenbrand, *The Crusades: Islamic Perspectives*

this angry desire for "revenge," but she believed these emotions and their outlet in mob violence, mainly against European Jews, did not end with the departure of the Crusader armies. Instead, she maintained, the violence actually worsened as the twelfth century continued.

Elsewhere, the historian Christopher Tyerman,* a former student of Riley-Smith's, rejected the idea that a military campaign simply needed the pope's approval to be called a "Crusade."[3] Since the term Crusade was only invented later, one could not call the campaign of 1096–99 the First "Crusade" if the people who were there did not do so. While not an outright rejection of Riley-Smith's line of thought, this nevertheless seriously questioned his argument that the First Crusade was the "pivot" around which the very concept of Christian warfare turned.

The foremost traditionalist historian Hans Eberhard Mayer spoke respectfully about Riley-Smith's views in a 1988 edition of his work *The Crusades* (originally published in German in 1965). But he was careful to present evidence for both sides of the argument throughout his additions. He admitted that he had not yet actually read *The First Crusade* at the time of writing.[4] His own view remained that the capture of Jerusalem was always the main goal of the Crusade, with religious devotion and the wish to do penance —the two reasons Riley-Smith found so important—only coming second.

Responses

The First Crusade provided an important alternative view, supporting the pluralist argument that any military campaign approved by the pope was a Crusade; Riley-Smith became arguably its most respected advocate. In reviewing Christopher Tyerman's *The Debate on the Crusades* (2011) in the paper "Issues of Historiography," Simon John of the University of Swansea called the network of Crusades scholars in Cambridge and London "the Jonathan Riley-Smith school." He referred to *The First Crusade* as a standard text on numerous aspects of early Crusading.[5]

For his part, Riley-Smith has admitted that his text has been "controversial," though he did not go into details about who might find it so. In the 2009 edition, he accepted Susanna Throop's criticisms of his earlier claim that feelings of vengeance toward European Jews peaked in the years of the First Crusade and declined thereafter. Throop had disputed that position, stating that these violent outbursts did not end with the First Crusade and were likely a sign of a deeper prejudice. While Riley-Smith accepted that she was correct, he maintained that some among the knightly classes had understood Pope Urban's II's* preaching for the First Crusade to be a call for a vendetta against people they perceived to be enemies of the Church.[6] This encouraged them in their violent attacks against Jews and Muslims.

Although Riley-Smith and Christopher Tyerman had disagreed on the importance of the First Crusade in the development of Christian holy war, with Tyerman concluding that there were no actual Crusades until the reign of Pope Innocent III more than a century later, they remained on good terms. Riley-Smith gave a special place to Tyerman's opposing argument in the select bibliography of the second edition *The Crusades: A History* (2005).[7]

Conflict and Consensus

Given the number of different opinions among academics and the quantity of original sources for the early Crusades (including many waiting to be discovered), it seems unlikely that any agreement will be reached about the true nature of the First Crusade.

Fully two decades after the publication of *The First Crusade*, Riley-Smith was critiquing the findings of the historian Norman Housely's* *Contesting the Crusades* (2006). Riley-Smith noted that although both he and Housely could be counted among the pluralist* school of Crusade historians (to use Housely's term), they did not agree on everything. Nevertheless, Riley-Smith referred to Housely as "perceptive" and "brilliant," a mark of the mutual respect that exists among the members of what is in reality a very small club. By that time, both Housely and Riley-Smith were both doubtful about the value of the pluralist definition of a Crusade as any military campaign for which the pope gave his blessing, saying this definition was no longer the "panacea" (that is, the perfect solution) they once thought it to be.[8] Their doubts only deepened when Tyerman, one of Riley-Smith's followers, found that there had been no "official" papal approval for the First Crusade until a century after the campaign.

Traditionalist Crusade historians tend to view the medieval campaigns as motivated by religious fanaticism and the desire to plunder riches from the Holy Land. Yet in his review of Housely's work, Riley-Smith also noted the lack of a coherent traditionalist school in modern academia to oppose the pluralists. Some historians, like the English scholar Giles Constable* and Tyerman, were prepared to question some elements of pluralism. But they were also members of the pluralist group themselves, and so were hardly outright critics.

Riley-Smith seems almost disappointed that those academics who might make a case for the traditionalist view of the Crusades are, for whatever reason, reluctant to speak about it publicly. It is telling that the most well-known modern supporter of the traditionalist school, Hans Eberhard Mayer, is now in his eighties and his last major work to be published in English was originally written in the 1960s.[9]

NOTES

1   James Brundage, Review of *The First Crusade and the Idea of Crusading*, *The American Historical Review* 93, no 1 (1988): 227, accessed February 2, 2016, http://ahr.oxfordjournals.org/content/93/1/133.full.pdf+html.

2   Profile of James Brundage, *crusaderstudies*, accessed December 15, 2015, http://www.crusaderstudies.org.uk/resources/historians/profiles/brundage/index.html.

3   Christopher Tyerman, *The Invention of the Crusades*, (London: Palgrave Macmillan, 1998).

4   Hans Eberhard Mayer, *The Crusades*, 2nd ed. (Oxford: Oxford University Press, 1988), 292.

5   Simon John, Review of *The Debate on the Crusades, 1099–2010, Issues in Historiography*, review no. 1153, accessed December 11, 2015, http://www.history.ac.uk/reviews/review/1153.

6   Jonathan Riley-Smith, *The First Crusade and the Idea of Crusading*, 2nd ed. (London: Continuum, 2009), 6.

7   Jonathan Riley-Smith, *The Crusades: A History,* 2nd ed(London: Continuum, 2005), 310.

8   Jonathan Riley-Smith, Review of *Contesting the Crusades* by Norman Housely, *The Catholic Historical Review* Volume 93, no. 3: (2007), accessed December 15, 2015, https://muse.jhu.edu/login?auth=0&type=summary&url=/journals/catholic_historical_review/v093/93.3riley-smith.html.

9   Hans Eberhard Mayer, *The Crusades*.

MODULE 10
THE EVOLVING DEBATE

KEY POINTS

- *The First Crusade and the Idea of Crusading* had a considerable impact on the work of historians. It inspired other researchers to make use of the collections of Church documents from the time and to organize their data using new digital means.

- In the years following the book's publication, Jonathan Riley-Smith gained an international reputation as a nontraditionalist* scholar of the Crusades* and the foremost British historian of the period.

- While the pluralist* school, of which he is a leading member, overwhelmed the traditionalists, pluralist arguments are yet to make the same mark in the wider public sphere.

Uses and Problems

Most modern histories of the Crusades have used a combination of ideas that Jonathan Riley-Smith put forward in *The First Crusade and the Idea of Crusading*, published in 1986. All of the important Crusade books since then, whether intended for the growing nonacademic market or not, have built on the foundations of his work.

One of the first was the British historian John France's* *Victory in the East: A Military History of The First Crusade* (1996). In that book, for example, France identifies Riley-Smith's research on the nature of Jerusalem as a goal for Pope Urban II* when he began preaching the First Crusade* as a key contribution in the field.[1] Since then, Thomas F. Madden's* *The New Concise History of the Crusades* (1999) has adopted Riley-Smith's argument that the First Crusade* could be

> **66** There is talk of the re-emergence of holy war and the lasting effects of the Crusades between Christians and Muslims, even if the demonizing of the Crusaders by Muslims has much more to do with nationalist reactions to the West since the late nineteenth century. **99**
>
> Jonathan Riley-Smith, *The First Crusade: Origins and Impact*

divided into three distinct "waves." Christopher Tyerman's* *God's War: A New History of the Crusades* (2006) and Jonathan Phillips's* *Holy Warriors: A Modern History of the Crusades* (2009) have used Riley-Smith's theory of devotional war to build their own histories of how the Crusades came about. These historians have also followed Riley-Smith's lead both in making use of collections of handwritten Church documents for their research and using the digital methods of scholarship that he pioneered.

Schools of Thought

Riley-Smith can rightly lay claim to founding and leading two distinct but not opposing schools of thought. The first is the larger, international, pluralist school of Crusade scholars, whose members include American and British historians. He is also the leading British historian of the Crusades and one of the first authors to be read by undergraduates new to the topic or anyone simply interested in studying the Crusades.

The scholar Norman Housely* names him as the historian who provided a firm answer to Hans Eberhard Mayer's* call for a definition of what the Crusades actually were. Riley-Smith's answer was so convincing that it effectively ended Mayer's own traditionalist school. Housely states that all new advances in Crusade history in recent decades have come from Riley-Smith's influence. It is worth noting that when Housely reviewed Christopher Tyerman's *The Invention of* *the Crusades* for the journal *International History Review* in 1999, he used the first three paragraphs to discuss not Tyerman but Riley-Smith.[2]

Riley-Smith's reputation in British Crusade studies is such that his appeal for more Western scholars to work on the Crusades led the historian Carole Hillenbrand* to refocus her work. She learned Arabic* and relied solely on Islamic sources in her groundbreaking work *The Crusades: Islamic Perspectives* (1999).[3] Although this is an area in which Riley-Smith's contribution amounts to little more than moral support, his backing is important enough to be featured prominently on the book's cover and to merit numerous mentions in the prologue.

In Current Scholarship

Before the publication of *The First Crusade*, the traditionalist view of the Crusades still held sway over the majority of Crusade history writing. Today, the same could be said of Riley-Smith. Almost all of the general histories of the Crusades written during the past 20 years have been the work of historians closely allied to him in some form. Some, like Christopher Tyerman and Jonathan Phillips are former students. Others, like Carole Hillenbrand and Thomas Asbridge,* author of *The Crusades: War for the Holy Land* (2012), list him in their acknowledgements and, in Asbridge's case, cite him frequently.

At the same time, the Crusades have gained a new importance in the modern struggle against violent Islamism* (a form of radically politicized Islam influential among certain terrorist organizations). Arguments that were once used only by academics like Riley-Smith, Mayer, and Hillenbrand now appear in the mainstream media on an almost weekly basis. Riley-Smith himself was quoted widely in 2005 when he criticized the film *Kingdom of Heaven*,* set in the Levant* of the late twelfth century, as "utter nonsense" and "absolute balls" that pandered to Islamic fundamentalists and would likely fuel their anger;

the historian Jonathan Phillips echoed these views.[4] Another of Riley-Smith's colleagues, Thomas F. Madden, has been particularly outspoken in regard to the public portrayal of the Crusades, perhaps as a result of having access to the large American media outlets in his position as professor of history at Saint Louis University. He most recently denounced the many comparisons between medieval Crusaders and the terrorist group ISIS/Daesh.*[5]

NOTES

1   John France, *Victory in the East: A Military History of the First Crusade* (Cambridge: Cambridge University Press, 1994), 4.

2   Norman Housely, Review of *The Invention of the Crusades* by Christopher Tyerman *The International History Review* 21, no. 2 (1999), 455–7, accessed January 6 2016, http://www.jstor.org/stable/40109013?seq=1#page_scan_tab_contents.

3   Carole Hillenbrand, *The Crusades: Islamic Perspectives* (Edinburgh: Edinburgh University Press, 1999), 3.

4   Charlotte Edwardes, "Ridley Scott's New Film 'Panders to Osama bin Laden,'" *Daily Telegraph*, January 18, 2004, accessed Dec. 15 2015, http://www.telegraph.co.uk/news/worldnews/northamerica/usa/1452000/Ridley-Scotts-new-Crusades-film-panders-to-Osama-bin-Laden.html.

5   Thomas F. Madden, "The Islamic State Members Think They Are Fighting a New Crusade. They're Wrong," *Washington Post*, December 4, 2015, accessed December 15, 2015. https://www.washingtonpost.com/news/in-theory/wp/2015/12/04/the-islamic-states-members-believe-they-are-fighting-a-new-crusade-theyre-wrong/.

MODULE 11
IMPACT AND INFLUENCE TODAY

KEY POINTS

- As present-day turmoil has engulfed the Middle East and the West has considered its responses, *The First Crusade* has taken on a new relevance and importance.

- In the light of developments such as the rise of Islamism* and terrorism in the name of religion, much of what is described in the book seems almost familiar.

- Despite the fact that Riley-Smith and other scholars have shifted the understanding of the Crusades* within academic circles, public thinking has hardly changed.

Position

Although Jonathan Riley-Smith's colleagues and students have published a number of volumes on the First Crusade* in the past three decades, none of them has focused solely on the idea of Crusading, as described in Riley-Smith's *The First Crusade and the Idea of Crusading*. It remains the leading presentation of the medieval Crusader* mindset to this day. Considering how much attention has been focused on the Middle East and all the changes that have taken place in the 30 years since publication, this is a remarkable feat.

Following the events of the War on Terror,* the Arab Spring,* and the Syrian Civil War,* the Crusades have never been a more loaded topic in modern public discussion. And yet these recent events could be argued to have numbed audiences to a degree; it is hard to imagine the impact that the book must have had on those who came across it when it was first published. Religious conflict and the idea of holy war are nowadays sadly commonplace, even in parts of Europe once

> **"** The First Crusade was especially psychotic. **"**
>
> Karen Armstrong, *Fields of Blood: Religion and the History of Violence*

considered completely secular.* This was not the case in 1986 when Riley-Smith published *The First Crusade*. At that time, the idea that a war could be fought for reasons of religious faith was so outmoded as to be almost unthinkable. *The First Crusade* offers a new kind of relevance in an age marked by jihad* (the Islamic understanding of holy war) and the mindsets of those involved, while still alien to modern sensibilities, are, perhaps, familiar.

Interaction

Even though it began as an academic argument, the definition of what the Crusades were and why they occurred took on particular importance in the decades following the publication of *The First Crusade*. Riley-Smith may have sensed that things were about to change with the religiously fueled Iranian Revolution* of 1979 and the anti-Western sentiments of its new government. But he could hardly have guessed how things would turn out. The first time that hardline Islamic views on history and culture likely impacted Western populations was the fatwa,* or religious decree, issued in 1989 against the British novelist Salman Rushdie* by Iran's spiritual leader, Ayatollah Khomeini.

After the terror attacks of 9/11*, President George W. Bush* used the term "Crusade" to describe the fight against terrorism that America would mount. Only then did the full weight of the issue begin to sink in to a changed West and those searching for a reason for the violence began to look into the meaning and origins of the Crusades. Today the issue is as alive as it has ever been[1] and debates continue as to whether the Crusades were a spiritually inspired and devotional reaction to Islamic conquests in the Levant* (as Riley-Smith would have it) or aggressive in nature. In this context, *The First Crusade* remains a valuable guide for those who wish to learn.

The Continuing Debate

The motivations of the Crusades will continue to be a topic of debate into the future. Modern Islamic fundamentalists and terror groups refer to all Westerners as "Crusaders" and so the fascination with the topic can be expected to continue so long as those groups are active. The Crusades are also likely to be mentioned whenever the possibility of Western intervention in the Middle East is brought up.[2]

For over a decade, Riley-Smith and the historians Thomas F. Madden* and Carole Hillenbrand* have attempted to draw attention to the misunderstandings about this historical period—largely without success. In the academic world, they can revise the history of the Crusades and be guaranteed an audience. But the image of the supposed mindless barbarity of the First Crusade is so deeply engrained in public awareness that no fewer than two American presidents, Bill Clinton* and Barack Obama,* have publically repeated it. In such a situation, scholars' efforts to stop the spread of ill-informed ideas appear futile.

In the introduction to his own general history of the First Crusade in 2005, the British historian and writer Thomas Asbridge* wrote, "In its various incarnations over the past 150 years, the expedition has been all but stripped of its devotional context to become little more than a grand raid, presented as the first glorious flowering of western colonialism* and exposed as conclusive evidence of medieval Europe's spectacular barbarity…"[3] It was this devotional aspect that Riley-Smith attempted to restore in *The First Crusade*. It seems it will still be some time until the distinction is widely understood.

NOTES

1   Jonah Goldberg, "Horse Pucky from Obama." *National Review*, February 6, 2015, accessed December 15 2015, http://www.nationalreview.com/article/398030/horse-pucky-obama-jonah-goldberg.

2   Russ Read, "Rand Paul: Muslims Will Think 'Crusades Are Back' if US Puts Boots on the Ground." *Libertarian Republic*, December 9, 2015, accessed December 15, 2015, http://thelibertarianrepublic.com/rand-paul-muslims-will-think-crusades-are-back-if-us-puts-boots-on-the-ground/.

3   Thomas Asbridge, Preface to *The First Crusade: A New History: The Roots of Conflict between Christianity and Islam* (New York: Oxford University Press, 2004), xi.

MODULE 12
WHERE NEXT?

KEY POINTS

- The scholarship of *The First Crusade* demonstrates that no matter how much time has passed since an event, or how much has been written about it, there will always be something new to discover.

- Due to their ongoing relevance in current politics and international relations, Riley-Smith's positions on the meaning of the Crusades* and devotional war will continue to be debated for some time.

- *The First Crusade* provided an explanation and level of research into the origins of the Crusades that has yet to be bettered.

Potential

Jonathan Riley-Smith's body of work remains relevant and on the reading lists of leading universities in Britain and the United States. As such, *The First Crusade and the Idea of Crusading* could reasonably be expected to remain influential for many years to come. It has been widely cited in the books of other historians, and reviews of the work are always supportive of its status as a leading text on the issue. As the debate over the meaning of the Crusades continues, so will its relevance as an authoritative work on the origins and motives of Crusading. Despite the fact that it is a specialist text, it remains accessible to the undergraduate and the ordinary reader. Moreover, it charts in a very accessible way how a pope's somewhat ordinary appeal grew into a movement and a period of extraordinary importance in world history.

The only reason the book has not become more widely known among nonspecialists is that Riley-Smith has subsequently written a

> **❝** Professor Jonathan Riley-Smith proved important in formulating my ideas and tracking down various elusive sources. **❞**
>
> Jonathan Phillips, *The Fourth Crusade and the Sack of Constantinople*

number of general histories more commonly chosen by general readers. Despite the fact that a new edition of *The First Crusade* was published in 2009, the age of the text will count against it, and readers are likely to opt for one of the more up-to-date volumes on the subject, missing out on the unique collection of actual Crusader accounts, as unearthed from the cartularies,* that *The First Crusade* has to offer.

Future Directions

Luckily, Riley-Smith's former students are now established in both academia and the wider world, and they have helped make his name and work the leading authority on the topic of the Crusades and their origins. The historian Thomas F. Madden* praises Riley-Smith's ideas and methods of scholarship in his *New Concise History of the Crusades* (2005) and again in the book's latest edition in 2013.[1] Riley-Smith's former students, Thomas Asbridge* and Christopher Tyerman,* also feature their mentor's name prominently in their various works. Another of his colleagues, Carole Hillenbrand,* published a major new history of Islam in 2015.

Jonathan Phillips, a slightly younger former student, is professor of Crusading history at Royal Holloway, University of London, one of Riley-Smith's previous academic homes. Phillips is the coeditor of the academic journal *Crusades*, and contributes regularly to the BBC, the British public broadcaster.[2] He has written both general histories of the Crusades and more detailed treatments such as *Defenders of the Holy Land: Relations between the Latin East and West, 1119–1187* (1996). Phillips dedicated his book *The Crusades 1095–*

1204 (2002) to his former supervisor and it seems most likely that he will continue the work begun by Riley-Smith for a longer period into the future than his other followers.

Summary

Students should read *The First Crusades* to reach a greater understanding of the principles of research and the importance of a creative approach in seeking answers to research questions. Its pages contain a wealth of information for the beginner historian, and its style and the fact that it is a relatively short text are a lesson in economy of language. Simultaneously, its explanation of the origins and development of the Crusading movement, whose global impact is still felt today, has yet to be bettered; certainly its arguments have not been overturned.

When *The First Crusade* was published, our understanding of the history of the Crusades had been largely stagnant for three decades. With a novel and exacting approach, however, Jonathan Riley-Smith managed to reinvent that history. Though he could not have foreseen it, Crusader scholarship is today in good health, and those who study it are often called upon to comment and explain the past in outlets that would once have been completely closed off to the medieval historian. Much of the cause of this newfound acceptance has its roots in the turmoil in the Middle East and the tragic events of the last 15 years. But it is a testament to Riley-Smith's ability that so much has been done for the subject in that time.

NOTES

1   Thomas F. Madden, *The New Concise History of the Crusades* (Baltimore: Rowman and Littlefield, 2005), 217.

2   Profile of Jonathan Phillips, Royal Holloway, University of London, accessed December 15, 2015, https://pure.royalholloway.ac.uk/portal/en/persons/jonathan-phillips_b03e8695-cb27-4488-b5a0-80af2e5b3d77.html.

GLOSSARY

GLOSSARY OF TERMS

Antioch, Siege of: a hard-fought battle between the forces of the First Crusade and the Islamic defenders of Antioch, a city in today's southern Turkey, as well as those of the surrounding cities Damascus and Aleppo, between 1097 and 1098. The Crusaders only managed to take most of the city after a long siege, but were then surrounded themselves by a Muslim relief force. A surprise attack broke this last siege and the Crusaders took the city.

Arabic: the principal language of the Muslim Middle East during the Crusades. Most surviving documents from this period were written in Arabic. The language remains dominant in large areas of the modern Middle East and North Africa.

Arab Spring: a widely used term to describe a series of protests and revolutions that began in North Africa in 2010, spreading throughout the Middle East. These events have been widespread and have led to changes of ruler in Tunisia, Egypt, Libya, and Yemen.

Byzantine Empire: the successor state to the Eastern Roman Empire. The Byzantines were engaged in a series of conflicts with various Muslim states during this period. The Orthodox Christian Byzantine Empire often came into conflict with the Roman Catholic Crusaders.

Capitalism: an economic system in which a country's economy is controlled by private owners for their profit. The government generally plays some role in regulating economic activity and, in some countries, may own some industries, especially power, water, and communications utilities.

Cartularies: handwritten Church documents such as title deeds and wills.

Catholic: the Church and followers of the Roman Catholic religion, the largest single-faith domination in the world, whose spiritual leader is the pope.

Christian liberation movement: also known as liberation theology, this was a pan-South American Roman Catholic movement started in the 1950s that sought to address government abuse of power, injustice, and poverty. Based on their reading of the Bible, some participants supported the use of violence.

Colonialism: the annexation of one area or state by another for the reason of economic or strategic gain.

Communism: an ideology developed mainly from the theories of Karl Marx that holds that the ideal society is one in which all property and means of production are held in common ownership, recognizing neither nationalistic, racial, nor religious differences among peoples.

Council of Clermont: the site of a large ecumenical (Church) council called by Pope Urban II in 1095. The popular story goes that Urban preached there to urge knights and great men of France to travel to the East and regain Jerusalem in what would become the First Crusade.

Crusader orders of knights (also Crusading orders and knightly orders): a number of semi-monastic bodies founded in the wake of the First Crusade that policed the Crusader states, protecting Christian pilgrims and offering them aid where needed. Eventually, some of these groups, like the Knights Templar and Knights Hospitaller, became international organizations and military forces in their own right, with interests in banking and property.

Crusaders: Christian combatants in the Crusades.

Crusader states: a number of Roman Catholic governed principalities founded during and after the First Crusade, which ran from northern Syria, along the Levantine coast, down to Sinai, Egypt, in the south. The largest of these was the Kingdom of Jerusalem.

Crusades: by the most narrow definition, a series of religiously motivated invasions of the Levant by European Christians between 1096 and 1291. Broader definitions include holy wars against Muslims in other areas such as Iberia and Sicily, pagans in the Baltic region, other Christians such as the Byzantines and Russians, and Christian holy wars outside this period.

Doryleum, Battle of: a town in northwestern Anatolia (now Turkey), where a large scale ambush by the Seljuk Turks on the forces of the First Crusade occurred in 1097. The Crusaders were successful in repulsing the attack and even managed to capture the Seljuk ruler's camp and treasury after putting the Turks to flight.

Fatwa: a judgement or ruling in Islamic law made by a trained party. The term became popular in the Western world after a sentence of death was passed in 1989 on the novelist Salman Rushdie by the Ayatollah Khomeini of Iran following the publication of Rushdie's book *The Satanic Verses*.

First Crusade: a massive, religiously motivated, military invasion of the Levant by Christians from across Western Europe between 1096 and 1099. The most successful of all the Crusades from a military perspective, the First Crusade resulted in the establishment of the Crusader states in the Levant.

Franks: in relation to the Crusades, the term "Franks" refers to the Crusaders in general rather than any specific nationality. Many of the Crusaders were from France (Francia).

Gesta Francorum: (literally, the Deeds of the Franks), a historical account of the First Crusade written during and/or immediately after the event, most likely by a French-speaking South Italian Norman.

Historiography: the study of how history is written and recorded. In essence, the history of history.

Imperialism: traditionally refers to the Western military, political, and economic dominance of other areas of the world. In the modern world, the term usually carries negative connotations and is used to criticize Western interference in other countries.

Iranian hostage crisis: a 1979 incident when 52 members of the United States embassy and some non-embassy staff in Tehran were taken hostage by elements of the student armed forces supporting the Iranian Revolution. They were eventually released more than a year later.

Iranian Revolution: a series of strikes and mass demonstrations beginning in late 1977 against the royal regime of the Shah of Iran, which eventually led to his exile and overthrow in 1979. A new theocratic government under the leadership of the formerly exiled Ayatollah Khomeini introduced strict regulations requiring adherence to Islamic law, and Iran became the world's first official "Islamic Republic" thereafter.

Iraq War (2003–11): a conflict that started with an invasion of Iraq by a United States-led coalition, leading to the deposing of the Iraqi dictator, Saddam Hussein. After the war, coalition forces occupied Iraq until 2011, during which time they had to fight a sporadic insurgency.

ISIS/Daesh/Islamic State (of Iraq and Syria): a radical Islamist militant group that seized control of large swathes of territory in Iraq and Syria in 2014, and is also known to operate in eastern Libya, the Sinai Peninsula of Egypt, and other areas of the Middle East and North Africa.

Islamism: an ideology that calls for the introduction and use of Islamic religious law throughout all aspects of public and private life.

Jerusalem, Battle of: the capture in 1099 of the city of Jerusalem by the forces of the First Crusade. It would remain in Western European possession for less than a century, when the forces of the Kurdish sultan, Saladin, recaptured it after a siege in 1187.

Jihad: in the context of the Crusades (and modern conflict), the term almost invariably refers to "lesser jihad," the physical struggle against opponents of Islam, as opposed to "greater jihad," the inner spiritual struggle within every believer to fulfill his religious duties. During the Crusading period, jihad was seen as a defensive holy war to reclaim the Holy Land from the invading Crusaders.

Ruhollah Khomeini (1902–89) was an Iranian Shia Muslim religious leader, the founder and leader of the Islamic Republic of Iran in 1979. Known in the West as Ayatollah Khomeini, he notoriously called for the assassination of the novelist Salman Rushdie in 1989.

Kingdom of Heaven: a 2005 motion picture directed by Ridley Scott and written by William Monahan. Although the makers of the film maintained that the events shown were factual and a true representation of life in Europe and the Crusader states in the late twelfth century, the movie was heavily criticized by a number of medieval historians.

Knights Hospitaller: a hybrid military and religious order established to provide protection for Christian pilgrims to the Holy Land and care for the sick following the First Crusade in 1099 (though elements of the order were known to be in existence up to eight decades before). The order survived the end of the Crusade and modern groups are still in existence that claim descent from the medieval predecessor.

Levant: a vaguely defined region to the east of the Mediterranean. It consists primarily of modern-day Syria, Lebanon, Israel, Jordan and the Palestinian Territories. Cyprus, Iraq, Turkey and Egypt are sometimes included in this region.

Materialist: a school of thought in Crusade historiography that maintains that the primary motivation of the Crusades was the promise of captured land and treasure, rather than religiously inspired intentions.

Marxism: an ideology based on the teachings of Karl Marx, a nineteenth-century German political philosopher and economist, who developed a system of economic and historical analysis of society and is considered the father of modern communism.

Medieval period: also known as the Middle Ages, the period between the fall of the Roman Empire in the West (traditionally dated 476 C.E.) and the resurgence of Classical art and humanist philosophy during the Renaissance (traditionally late 1300s).

Middle Ages: the classification used to denote the period between the fall of the Roman Empire in Western Europe (traditionally dated as 476 C.E.) and the European Renaissance ("Rebirth") around 1350.

Middle East: the geographic region roughly containing modern Turkey, Lebanon, Syria, Israel, the Palestinian Territories, Egypt, the Arabian Peninsula, Jordan, Iraq, and Iran.

Munich Olympics: during the Summer Olympics of 1972 in the southern German city of Munich, members of the Palestinian Black September group infiltrated the athletes' village and took the Israeli team hostage, killing two members in the process. Nine more Israelis were killed, along with five of their captors and a West German policeman, when the security forces attempted an armed rescue.

Nazi: the shorthand term for the National Socialist German Workers' Party, which was led by Adolf Hitler and ruled Germany from 1933 to 1945. In modern times, it has come to be a pejorative term for far right or authoritarian groups and individuals across the English-speaking world.

9/11: a series of attacks made on September 11, 2001, against the United States by the terrorist organization al-Qaeda. Three passenger aircraft were hijacked and flown into the twin towers of the World Trade Center in New York and the Pentagon outside Washington DC. A fourth aircraft was hijacked and targeted the Capitol in Washington but crashed after its passengers attempted to overcome the hijackers.

Penance: a Roman Catholic practice in which an individual carries out some devotional or charitable deed to seek forgiveness for past sins.

Pluralist school: a school of thought within Crusade scholarship that questions traditionalist views that the Crusades were a limited number of campaigns directed against Islamic Middle Eastern powers, largely undertaken for the motive of acquiring land and treasures.

Protestant: a Christian Church that emerged during the Reformation in the sixteenth century. It denies the authority of the pope and places emphasis on Biblical truth and a personalized faith.

Reconquista: the centuries-long war by Catholic forces to retake Spain and Portugal from the Arab Islamic forces who had invaded in the early eighth century. The era came to an end in 1492 with the fall of the last Islamic state, Granada.

Reformation: the movement that began in the early sixteenth century as a succession of protests against the policies of the Catholic Church. Eventually, large numbers of Catholics, mainly in northern Europe, broke away from the Church and formed their own congregations. This development initiated large-scale reforms within the Catholic Church itself, as well as the outbreak of religious wars in some areas.

Revisionist history: the reassessment and sometimes rewriting of historical events in a way that differs from the previous, commonly accepted, narrative.

Roman Empire: an ancient state that grew originally from the city of Rome in central Italy to rule the entire Mediterranean region and areas of northern Europe. At its height, in the first and second centuries, the Empire's borders stretched from southern Scotland to Iraq, and its ongoing influence in Western culture is still seen in language, religion, and architecture. Though the western half was replaced by successor states by 500 C.E., its eastern provinces continued an unbroken line of government until 1453, a state now described as the Byzantine Empire.

Secular: without religious or spiritual influence, particularly at the level of the state.

Syrian Civil War: an ongoing conflict fought between the Syrian government and assorted insurgent groups. Various forms of unilateral and cooperative interference by the governments and forces of other countries have been widespread, and the conflict has created millions of refugees fleeing the fighting.

Traditionalist: a school of thought within Crusade historiography that holds that the Crusades were undertaken for nefarious motives, namely land, wealth, and power. Another common aspect of the traditionalist school concentrates on the violence of the Crusades, which proponents claim was excessive and of a particularly cruel nature.

The "Troubles": the term used to describe the frequently violent conflict in Ireland provoked by nationalist sentiment and questions over the status of the British territory of Northern Ireland from 1969 to 1998.

War on Terror: the name used to refer to the military campaigns in various locations around the world led by the United States following the September 11, 2001 terrorist attacks.

World War II (1939–45): global conflict that pitted the Axis Powers of Nazi Germany, Fascist Italy and Imperial Japan against the Allied nations including Britain, the United States and the USSR.

Yugoslavia: a country created in the wake of World War I from a collection of Slavic majority areas and states in the southeastern Balkan area of Europe. Dominated by Serbia, its break-up in the late 1980s and early 1990s led to violent, sometimes genocidal, civil wars.

PEOPLE MENTIONED IN THE TEXT

Alexander the Great (356–323 B.C.E.) was a Macedonian leader whose conquest of the Persian Empire and parts of India in the fourth century B.C.E. led to the spread of classical Greek culture throughout the Middle East and beyond.

Thomas Asbridge (b. 1969) is a historian, writer, and television presenter. The author of *The Greatest Knight: The Remarkable Life of William Marshal, the Power Behind Five English Thrones* (2014) and *The Crusades* (2010), he wrote and presented the BBC Two documentary *The Greatest Knight: William the Marshal.*

Augustine of Hippo (354–430) was a North African Christian bishop and philosopher. His works, particularly the *City of God* (426), are foundational works of Christian theology.

Baldric of Bourgueil (circa 1050–1130) was abbot of Bourgueil from 1079 to 1106, then bishop of Dol-en-Bretagne until his death. A poet, and scholar, he is noted as a historian of the First Crusade.

Geoffrey Barraclough (1908–84) was a British scholar who initially focused on medieval Germany and the papacy. He subsequently became a major commentator on contemporary history and the use of history within the social sciences.

Hugh Bochard was an eleventh-century Frankish knight who took part in the First Crusade. There is little record of his life other than that kept by his local church, where he mortgaged and sold many of his possessions to pay his expenses for the journey to the Holy Land.

George W. Bush (b. 1946) was the 43rd president of the United States. A Republican, he served two terms, from 2001 to 2009.

William Jefferson "Bill" Clinton (b.1946) was the 42nd president of the United States, whose two terms of office fell between 1993 and 2001. A member of the Democratic Party.

Alexius I Comnenus (1056–1118) was a Byzantine emperor whose appeal for Western assistance in the wake of massive encroachments of his territory led to the formation of the First Crusade.

Giles Constable (b. 1929) is an English historian of the Crusades and professor of history at both Harvard and Princeton.

John France (b. 1941) is a historian of the Crusades and military history and dean of the department of history and classics at Swansea University.

Edward Gibbon (1737–94) was an English writer and historian best known for his mammoth work *The History of the Decline and Fall of the Roman Empire* (1776).

Godfrey of Bouillon (1060–1100) was the Frankish Lord of Bouillon and Duke of Lower Lorraine. He played an integral role in the First Crusade and was made the first ruler of the new Kingdom of Jerusalem following the city's capture in 1099.

Guibert of Nogent (circa 1055–1124) was a Frankish monk of the Benedictine order who wrote a contemporary history of the First Crusade. This text, and his later autobiography, serve as important records of the time.

Carole Hillenbrand (b. 1943) is a British historian and professor of Islamic history at the University of Edinburgh since 2000. Her book *The Crusades: Islamic Perspectives* (1999) remains the largest single collection of historical Islamic sources on the Crusading era.

Norman Housely (b. 1952) is a historian of the Crusades and a professor of history at the University of Leicester. A close collaborator and former student of Jonathan Riley-Smith, he is credited with coining the term "pluralist" to describe the new, nontraditional historians of the Crusades who began publishing in the 1970s.

Martin Luther (1483–1546) was a German cleric whose protests against the policies of the Roman Catholic Church led to a mass movement and the breakaway of large numbers of northern Europeans from Catholicism.

Thomas F. Madden (b. 1960) is an American historian at Saint Louis University, whose work focuses on the Crusades.

Hans Eberhard Mayer (b. 1932) is an influential German historian of the Crusades and professor of medieval and modern history at the University of Kiel.

Barack Obama (b. 1961) is the 44th President of the United States, in office since 2009. He is leader of the Democratic Party.

Otbert of Liege was Bishop of Liege during the period immediately before and after the First Crusade, reputedly dying in 1119. He supported the intention of Duke Godfrey of Bouillon to take part in the Crusade by buying the Duke's duchy and providing him with ready cash, though he did not travel to the Holy Land himself, observing the Pope's decree banning churchmen from taking an active part in the campaign.

Jonathan Phillips (b. 1965) is a historian of the Crusades. His most recent work considers the relevance of the Crusades to the modern world.

Raynald Porchet was a Frankish knight of the First Crusade who was captured by the Islamic forces of Antioch in March 1098. After refusing to plead for ransom from his comrades, Porchet was offered significant rewards to convert from Christianity to Islam. After refusing once more, he was beheaded on the order of the garrison's commander. His story inspired a cult following and he was proclaimed a martyr.

Robert the Monk (d. 1122) was a twelfth century Frankish monk who rewrote and added to the *Gesta Francorum* of the First Crusade.

Robert of Normandy (1051–1134) was Duke of Normandy and eldest son of William the Conqueror of England. He mortgaged his duchy to his brother William II of England, before participating in the First Crusade in 1096. By the time of Robert's return in 1100, the throne of England had passed to his brother, now Henry I, and Robert launched a rebellion. He was unsuccessful and was imprisoned for over a quarter of a century. Normandy was absorbed as a possession of the English crown.

Jean Barthélémy Richard (b. 1921) is a French historian. A member of the *Institut de France* and former president of the prestigious *Académie des Inscriptions et Belles-Lettres*, he is a specialist in medieval history and has written extensively on the Crusades.

Steven Runciman (1903–2000) was a British historian specializing in the Crusades. His seminal work, a three-volume *History of the Crusades* (1951–54), was very influential within its field throughout the second half of the twentieth century and remains a valuable resource for modern students of the Crusades. His work has been criticized as outdated and Eurocentric by some recent authors.

Salman Rushdie (b. 1947) is an Anglo-Indian writer whose book *Midnight's Children* (1981) was proclaimed the best winner of all time by the Booker Prize in 2008. The contents of his 1988 book *The Satanic Verses* led to the imposition of a death sentence by the Ayatollah Khomeini for blasphemy.

Susanna Throop is an associate professor of medieval history at Ursinus College in Collegeville, Pennsylvania, and a former student of Jonathan Riley-Smith. She is the author of *Crusading as an Act of Vengeance, 1095–1216* (2011).

Christopher Tyerman (b. 1953) is a British professor of history at Hertford College, Oxford. He is best known for *God's War: A New History of the Crusades* (2006).

Pope Urban II (circa 1042–99) was the leader of the European Church from 1088 until 1099 and is best known for ending the Investiture Controversy with the German Emperor Henry IV and for calling for the First Crusade after an appeal for assistance by the Byzantine Emperor Alexius I Comnenus.

Voltaire (1694–1778) was the pseudonym of French writer Francois-Marie Arouet. He was an open critic of the French political and religious institutions of his day, and his ideas are believed to have had an influence in the outbreak of the French Revolution in 1789.

William the Conqueror (1028–87) was the Duke of Normandy and conqueror of England following his invasion in 1066, after a succession dispute arose with the reigning Saxon King of England, Harold Godwinson.

WORKS CITED

WORKS CITED

Asbridge, Thomas. *The First Crusade: A New History: The Roots of Conflict between Christianity and Islam*. New York: Oxford University Press, 2004.

Barber, Malcolm. *The Crusader States*. New Haven: Yale University Press, 2012.

Barraclough, Geoffrey. "Deus le Volt?" *New York Review of Books*, May 21, 1970. Accessed January 6, 2016. http://www.nybooks.com/articles/1970/05/21/deus-le-volt/.

Boyd, Kelly, ed. *Encyclopedia of Historians and Historical Writing, Volume 1*. London: Routledge, 1999.

Brundage, James. Review of *The First Crusade and the Idea of Crusading*. *American Historical Review* 93, no 1 (1988): 227. Accessed February 2, 2016. http://ahr.oxfordjournals.org/content/93/1/133.full.pdf+html.

Duffy, Eamon. "The Holy Terror." *New York Review of Books*. October 19, 2006. Accessed December 16, 2015. http://www.nybooks.com/articles/2006/10/19/the-holy-terror/.

Edwardes, Charlotte. "Ridley Scott's New Film 'Panders to Osama Bin Laden'." *Daily Telegraph*, January 18, 2004. Accessed December 15. 2015. http://www.telegraph.co.uk/news/worldnews/northamerica/usa/1452000/Ridley-Scotts-new-Crusades-film-panders-to-Osama-bin-Laden.html.

France, John. *Victory in the East: A Military History of the First Crusade*. Cambridge: Cambridge University Press, 1994.

Goldberg, Jonah. "Horse Pucky from Obama." *National Review*, February 6, 2015. Accessed December 15, 2015. http://www.nationalreview.com/article/398030/horse-pucky-obama-jonah-goldberg.

Hillenbrand, Carole. *The Crusades: Islamic Perspectives*. Edinburgh: Edinburgh University Press, 1999.

Holt, Andrew. "Crusades Were a Reaction to Militant Islam." *Jacksonville.com*, February 10 2015. Accessed 15 December, 2015. http://jacksonville.com/business/columnists/2015–02-10/story/guest-column-crusades-were-reaction-islamic-militarism.

Housely, Norman. Review of *The Invention of the Crusades* by Christopher Tyerman, *International History Review* 21, no. 2 (1999): 455-7. Accessed January 6, 2016. http://www.jstor.org/stable/40109013?seq=1#page_scan_tab_contents.

John, Arit. "Why the Crusades Still Matter." *Bloomberg Politics*, February 6, 2015. Accessed December 15, 2015. http://www.bloomberg.com/politics/articles/2015–02-06/why-the-crusades-still-matter.

John, Simon. Review of The Debate on the Crusades, 1099–2010. Issues in Historiography, review no. 1153. Accessed Dec. 11, 2015. http://www.history.ac.uk/reviews/review/1153.

Madden, Thomas F. "The Islamic State Members Think They Are Fighting a New Crusade. They're Wrong." *Washington Post*, December 4, 2015. Accessed December 15, 2015. https://www.washingtonpost.com/news/in-theory/wp/2015/12/04/the-islamic-states-members-believe-they-are-fighting-a-new-crusade-theyre-wrong/.

The New Concise History of the Crusades. Baltimore: Rowman and Littlefield, 2006.

Mayer, Hans Eberhard. *The Crusades*, 2nd ed. Oxford: Oxford University Press, 1988.

Michaelson, Jay. "The Crusades Were Great Actually!" *Daily Beast*, October 2, 2015. Accessed 15 Dec. 2015. http://www.thedailybeast.com/articles/2015/02/10/the-crusades-were-great-actually.html.

Phillips, Jonathan. "The Call of the Crusades." *History Today* 59, no.11 (2009). Accessed January 6, 2016. http://www.historytoday.com/jonathan-phillips/call-crusades.

Holy Warriors: A Modern History of the Crusades, London: Bodley Head, 2009.

Read, Russ. "Rand Paul: Muslims Will Think 'Crusades Are Back' if US Puts Boots on the Ground'." *The Libertarian Republic*, December 9, 2015. Accessed December 15, 2015. http://thelibertarianrepublic.com/rand-paul-muslims-will-think-crusades-are-back-if-us-puts-boots-on-the-ground/.

Riley-Smith, Jonathan. *The Crusades: A History*. 2nd ed. London: Continuum, 2005.

"Crusading as an Act of Love." *History* 65 (1980): 177–92. Reprinted in Thomas F. Madden, *The Crusades: The Essential Readings*, Oxford: Blackwell, 2002.

The First Crusade and the Idea of Crusading. 2nd ed. New York: Continuum, 2009.

The First Crusaders 1095–1131. Cambridge: Cambridge University Press, 1997.

Introduction to *The First Crusade: Origins and Impact*. Edited by Jonathan Phillips. Manchester: Manchester University Press, 1997.

Review of *Contesting the Crusades* by Norman Housely, *The Catholic Historical Review* 93, no. 3 (2007). Accessed December 15, 2015. https://muse.jhu.edu/login?auth=0&type=summary&url=/journals/catholic_historical_review/v093/93.3riley-smith.html.

What Were the Crusades? Basingstoke: Macmillan, 1977.

Riley-Smith, Jonathan, and Louise Riley-Smith. *The Crusades: Idea and Reality 1095–127.* London: Edward Arnold, 1981.

Royal Holloway, University of London. Profile of Professor Jonathan Phillips. Accessed December 15, 2015. https://pure.royalholloway.ac.uk/portal/en/persons/jonathan-phillips_b03e8695-cb27-4488-b5a0-80af2e5b3d77.html.

Tyerman, Christopher. *The Invention of the Crusades.* London: Palgrave Macmillan, 1998.

THE MACAT LIBRARY
BY DISCIPLINE

AFRICANA STUDIES

Chinua Achebe's *An Image of Africa: Racism in Conrad's Heart of Darkness*
W. E. B. Du Bois's *The Souls of Black Folk*
Zora Neale Huston's *Characteristics of Negro Expression*
Martin Luther King Jr's *Why We Can't Wait*
Toni Morrison's *Playing in the Dark: Whiteness in the American Literary Imagination*

ANTHROPOLOGY

Arjun Appadurai's *Modernity at Large: Cultural Dimensions of Globalisation*
Philippe Ariès's *Centuries of Childhood*
Franz Boas's *Race, Language and Culture*
Kim Chan & Renée Mauborgne's *Blue Ocean Strategy*
Jared Diamond's *Guns, Germs & Steel: the Fate of Human Societies*
Jared Diamond's *Collapse: How Societies Choose to Fail or Survive*
E. E. Evans-Pritchard's *Witchcraft, Oracles and Magic Among the Azande*
James Ferguson's *The Anti-Politics Machine*
Clifford Geertz's *The Interpretation of Cultures*
David Graeber's *Debt: the First 5000 Years*
Karen Ho's *Liquidated: An Ethnography of Wall Street*
Geert Hofstede's *Culture's Consequences: Comparing Values, Behaviors, Institutes and Organizations across Nations*
Claude Lévi-Strauss's *Structural Anthropology*
Jay Macleod's *Ain't No Makin' It: Aspirations and Attainment in a Low-Income Neighborhood*
Saba Mahmood's *The Politics of Piety: The Islamic Revival and the Feminist Subject*
Marcel Mauss's *The Gift*

BUSINESS

Jean Lave & Etienne Wenger's *Situated Learning*
Theodore Levitt's *Marketing Myopia*
Burton G. Malkiel's *A Random Walk Down Wall Street*
Douglas McGregor's *The Human Side of Enterprise*
Michael Porter's *Competitive Strategy: Creating and Sustaining Superior Performance*
John Kotter's *Leading Change*
C. K. Prahalad & Gary Hamel's *The Core Competence of the Corporation*

CRIMINOLOGY

Michelle Alexander's *The New Jim Crow: Mass Incarceration in the Age of Colorblindness*
Michael R. Gottfredson & Travis Hirschi's *A General Theory of Crime*
Richard Herrnstein & Charles A. Murray's *The Bell Curve: Intelligence and Class Structure in American Life*
Elizabeth Loftus's *Eyewitness Testimony*
Jay Macleod's *Ain't No Makin' It: Aspirations and Attainment in a Low-Income Neighborhood*
Philip Zimbardo's *The Lucifer Effect*

ECONOMICS

Janet Abu-Lughod's *Before European Hegemony*
Ha-Joon Chang's *Kicking Away the Ladder*
David Brion Davis's *The Problem of Slavery in the Age of Revolution*
Milton Friedman's *The Role of Monetary Policy*
Milton Friedman's *Capitalism and Freedom*
David Graeber's *Debt: the First 5000 Years*
Friedrich Hayek's *The Road to Serfdom*
Karen Ho's *Liquidated: An Ethnography of Wall Street*

John Maynard Keynes's *The General Theory of Employment, Interest and Money*
Charles P. Kindleberger's *Manias, Panics and Crashes*
Robert Lucas's *Why Doesn't Capital Flow from Rich to Poor Countries?*
Burton G. Malkiel's *A Random Walk Down Wall Street*
Thomas Robert Malthus's *An Essay on the Principle of Population*
Karl Marx's *Capital*
Thomas Piketty's *Capital in the Twenty-First Century*
Amartya Sen's *Development as Freedom*
Adam Smith's *The Wealth of Nations*
Nassim Nicholas Taleb's *The Black Swan: The Impact of the Highly Improbable*
Amos Tversky's & Daniel Kahneman's *Judgment under Uncertainty: Heuristics and Biases*
Mahbub Ul Haq's *Reflections on Human Development*
Max Weber's *The Protestant Ethic and the Spirit of Capitalism*

FEMINISM AND GENDER STUDIES

Judith Butler's *Gender Trouble*
Simone De Beauvoir's *The Second Sex*
Michel Foucault's *History of Sexuality*
Betty Friedan's *The Feminine Mystique*
Saba Mahmood's *The Politics of Piety: The Islamic Revival and the Feminist Subject*
Joan Wallach Scott's *Gender and the Politics of History*
Mary Wollstonecraft's *A Vindication of the Rights of Women*
Virginia Woolf's *A Room of One's Own*

GEOGRAPHY

The Brundtland Report's *Our Common Future*
Rachel Carson's *Silent Spring*
Charles Darwin's *On the Origin of Species*
James Ferguson's *The Anti-Politics Machine*
Jane Jacobs's *The Death and Life of Great American Cities*
James Lovelock's *Gaia: A New Look at Life on Earth*
Amartya Sen's *Development as Freedom*
Mathis Wackernagel & William Rees's *Our Ecological Footprint*

HISTORY

Janet Abu-Lughod's *Before European Hegemony*
Benedict Anderson's *Imagined Communities*
Bernard Bailyn's *The Ideological Origins of the American Revolution*
Hanna Batatu's *The Old Social Classes And The Revolutionary Movements Of Iraq*
Christopher Browning's *Ordinary Men: Reserve Police Batallion 101 and the Final Solution in Poland*
Edmund Burke's *Reflections on the Revolution in France*
William Cronon's *Nature's Metropolis: Chicago And The Great West*
Alfred W. Crosby's *The Columbian Exchange*
Hamid Dabashi's *Iran: A People Interrupted*
David Brion Davis's *The Problem of Slavery in the Age of Revolution*
Nathalie Zemon Davis's *The Return of Martin Guerre*
Jared Diamond's *Guns, Germs & Steel: the Fate of Human Societies*
Frank Dikotter's *Mao's Great Famine*
John W Dower's *War Without Mercy: Race And Power In The Pacific War*
W. E. B. Du Bois's *The Souls of Black Folk*
Richard J. Evans's *In Defence of History*
Lucien Febvre's *The Problem of Unbelief in the 16th Century*
Sheila Fitzpatrick's *Everyday Stalinism*

Eric Foner's *Reconstruction: America's Unfinished Revolution, 1863-1877*
Michel Foucault's *Discipline and Punish*
Michel Foucault's *History of Sexuality*
Francis Fukuyama's *The End of History and the Last Man*
John Lewis Gaddis's *We Now Know: Rethinking Cold War History*
Ernest Gellner's *Nations and Nationalism*
Eugene Genovese's *Roll, Jordan, Roll: The World the Slaves Made*
Carlo Ginzburg's *The Night Battles*
Daniel Goldhagen's *Hitler's Willing Executioners*
Jack Goldstone's *Revolution and Rebellion in the Early Modern World*
Antonio Gramsci's *The Prison Notebooks*
Alexander Hamilton, John Jay & James Madison's *The Federalist Papers*
Christopher Hill's *The World Turned Upside Down*
Carole Hillenbrand's *The Crusades: Islamic Perspectives*
Thomas Hobbes's *Leviathan*
Eric Hobsbawm's *The Age Of Revolution*
John A. Hobson's *Imperialism: A Study*
Albert Hourani's *History of the Arab Peoples*
Samuel P. Huntington's *The Clash of Civilizations and the Remaking of World Order*
C. L. R. James's *The Black Jacobins*
Tony Judt's *Postwar: A History of Europe Since 1945*
Ernst Kantorowicz's *The King's Two Bodies: A Study in Medieval Political Theology*
Paul Kennedy's *The Rise and Fall of the Great Powers*
Ian Kershaw's *The "Hitler Myth": Image and Reality in the Third Reich*
John Maynard Keynes's *The General Theory of Employment, Interest and Money*
Charles P. Kindleberger's *Manias, Panics and Crashes*
Martin Luther King Jr's *Why We Can't Wait*
Henry Kissinger's *World Order: Reflections on the Character of Nations and the Course of History*
Thomas Kuhn's *The Structure of Scientific Revolutions*
Georges Lefebvre's *The Coming of the French Revolution*
John Locke's *Two Treatises of Government*
Niccolò Machiavelli's *The Prince*
Thomas Robert Malthus's *An Essay on the Principle of Population*
Mahmood Mamdani's *Citizen and Subject: Contemporary Africa And The Legacy Of Late Colonialism*
Karl Marx's *Capital*
Stanley Milgram's *Obedience to Authority*
John Stuart Mill's *On Liberty*
Thomas Paine's *Common Sense*
Thomas Paine's *Rights of Man*
Geoffrey Parker's *Global Crisis: War, Climate Change and Catastrophe in the Seventeenth Century*
Jonathan Riley-Smith's *The First Crusade and the Idea of Crusading*
Jean-Jacques Rousseau's *The Social Contract*
Joan Wallach Scott's *Gender and the Politics of History*
Theda Skocpol's *States and Social Revolutions*
Adam Smith's *The Wealth of Nations*
Timothy Snyder's *Bloodlands: Europe Between Hitler and Stalin*
Sun Tzu's *The Art of War*
Keith Thomas's *Religion and the Decline of Magic*
Thucydides's *The History of the Peloponnesian War*
Frederick Jackson Turner's *The Significance of the Frontier in American History*
Odd Arne Westad's *The Global Cold War: Third World Interventions And The Making Of Our Times*

LITERATURE

Chinua Achebe's *An Image of Africa: Racism in Conrad's Heart of Darkness*
Roland Barthes's *Mythologies*
Homi K. Bhabha's *The Location of Culture*
Judith Butler's *Gender Trouble*
Simone De Beauvoir's *The Second Sex*
Ferdinand De Saussure's *Course in General Linguistics*
T. S. Eliot's *The Sacred Wood: Essays on Poetry and Criticism*
Zora Neale Huston's *Characteristics of Negro Expression*
Toni Morrison's *Playing in the Dark: Whiteness in the American Literary Imagination*
Edward Said's *Orientalism*
Gayatri Chakravorty Spivak's *Can the Subaltern Speak?*
Mary Wollstonecraft's *A Vindication of the Rights of Women*
Virginia Woolf's *A Room of One's Own*

PHILOSOPHY

Elizabeth Anscombe's *Modern Moral Philosophy*
Hannah Arendt's *The Human Condition*
Aristotle's *Metaphysics*
Aristotle's *Nicomachean Ethics*
Edmund Gettier's *Is Justified True Belief Knowledge?*
Georg Wilhelm Friedrich Hegel's *Phenomenology of Spirit*
David Hume's *Dialogues Concerning Natural Religion*
David Hume's *The Enquiry for Human Understanding*
Immanuel Kant's *Religion within the Boundaries of Mere Reason*
Immanuel Kant's *Critique of Pure Reason*
Søren Kierkegaard's *The Sickness Unto Death*
Søren Kierkegaard's *Fear and Trembling*
C. S. Lewis's *The Abolition of Man*
Alasdair MacIntyre's *After Virtue*
Marcus Aurelius's *Meditations*
Friedrich Nietzsche's *On the Genealogy of Morality*
Friedrich Nietzsche's *Beyond Good and Evil*
Plato's *Republic*
Plato's *Symposium*
Jean-Jacques Rousseau's *The Social Contract*
Gilbert Ryle's *The Concept of Mind*
Baruch Spinoza's *Ethics*
Sun Tzu's *The Art of War*
Ludwig Wittgenstein's *Philosophical Investigations*

POLITICS

Benedict Anderson's *Imagined Communities*
Aristotle's *Politics*
Bernard Bailyn's *The Ideological Origins of the American Revolution*
Edmund Burke's *Reflections on the Revolution in France*
John C. Calhoun's *A Disquisition on Government*
Ha-Joon Chang's *Kicking Away the Ladder*
Hamid Dabashi's *Iran: A People Interrupted*
Hamid Dabashi's *Theology of Discontent: The Ideological Foundation of the Islamic Revolution in Iran*
Robert Dahl's *Democracy and its Critics*
Robert Dahl's *Who Governs?*
David Brion Davis's *The Problem of Slavery in the Age of Revolution*

Alexis De Tocqueville's *Democracy in America*
James Ferguson's *The Anti-Politics Machine*
Frank Dikotter's *Mao's Great Famine*
Sheila Fitzpatrick's *Everyday Stalinism*
Eric Foner's *Reconstruction: America's Unfinished Revolution, 1863-1877*
Milton Friedman's *Capitalism and Freedom*
Francis Fukuyama's *The End of History and the Last Man*
John Lewis Gaddis's *We Now Know: Rethinking Cold War History*
Ernest Gellner's *Nations and Nationalism*
David Graeber's *Debt: the First 5000 Years*
Antonio Gramsci's *The Prison Notebooks*
Alexander Hamilton, John Jay & James Madison's *The Federalist Papers*
Friedrich Hayek's *The Road to Serfdom*
Christopher Hill's *The World Turned Upside Down*
Thomas Hobbes's *Leviathan*
John A. Hobson's *Imperialism: A Study*
Samuel P. Huntington's *The Clash of Civilizations and the Remaking of World Order*
Tony Judt's *Postwar: A History of Europe Since 1945*
David C. Kang's *China Rising: Peace, Power and Order in East Asia*
Paul Kennedy's *The Rise and Fall of Great Powers*
Robert Keohane's *After Hegemony*
Martin Luther King Jr.'s *Why We Can't Wait*
Henry Kissinger's *World Order: Reflections on the Character of Nations and the Course of History*
John Locke's *Two Treatises of Government*
Niccolò Machiavelli's *The Prince*
Thomas Robert Malthus's *An Essay on the Principle of Population*
Mahmood Mamdani's *Citizen and Subject: Contemporary Africa And The Legacy Of Late Colonialism*
Karl Marx's *Capital*
John Stuart Mill's *On Liberty*
John Stuart Mill's *Utilitarianism*
Hans Morgenthau's *Politics Among Nations*
Thomas Paine's *Common Sense*
Thomas Paine's *Rights of Man*
Thomas Piketty's *Capital in the Twenty-First Century*
Robert D. Putman's *Bowling Alone*
John Rawls's *Theory of Justice*
Jean-Jacques Rousseau's *The Social Contract*
Theda Skocpol's *States and Social Revolutions*
Adam Smith's *The Wealth of Nations*
Sun Tzu's *The Art of War*
Henry David Thoreau's *Civil Disobedience*
Thucydides's *The History of the Peloponnesian War*
Kenneth Waltz's *Theory of International Politics*
Max Weber's *Politics as a Vocation*
Odd Arne Westad's *The Global Cold War: Third World Interventions And The Making Of Our Times*

POSTCOLONIAL STUDIES

Roland Barthes's *Mythologies*
Frantz Fanon's *Black Skin, White Masks*
Homi K. Bhabha's *The Location of Culture*
Gustavo Gutiérrez's *A Theology of Liberation*
Edward Said's *Orientalism*
Gayatri Chakravorty Spivak's *Can the Subaltern Speak?*

PSYCHOLOGY

Gordon Allport's *The Nature of Prejudice*
Alan Baddeley & Graham Hitch's *Aggression: A Social Learning Analysis*
Albert Bandura's *Aggression: A Social Learning Analysis*
Leon Festinger's *A Theory of Cognitive Dissonance*
Sigmund Freud's *The Interpretation of Dreams*
Betty Friedan's *The Feminine Mystique*
Michael R. Gottfredson & Travis Hirschi's *A General Theory of Crime*
Eric Hoffer's *The True Believer: Thoughts on the Nature of Mass Movements*
William James's *Principles of Psychology*
Elizabeth Loftus's *Eyewitness Testimony*
A. H. Maslow's *A Theory of Human Motivation*
Stanley Milgram's *Obedience to Authority*
Steven Pinker's *The Better Angels of Our Nature*
Oliver Sacks's *The Man Who Mistook His Wife For a Hat*
Richard Thaler & Cass Sunstein's *Nudge: Improving Decisions About Health, Wealth and Happiness*
Amos Tversky's *Judgment under Uncertainty: Heuristics and Biases*
Philip Zimbardo's *The Lucifer Effect*

SCIENCE

Rachel Carson's *Silent Spring*
William Cronon's *Nature's Metropolis: Chicago And The Great West*
Alfred W. Crosby's *The Columbian Exchange*
Charles Darwin's *On the Origin of Species*
Richard Dawkin's *The Selfish Gene*
Thomas Kuhn's *The Structure of Scientific Revolutions*
Geoffrey Parker's *Global Crisis: War, Climate Change and Catastrophe in the Seventeenth Century*
Mathis Wackernagel & William Rees's *Our Ecological Footprint*

SOCIOLOGY

Michelle Alexander's *The New Jim Crow: Mass Incarceration in the Age of Colorblindness*
Gordon Allport's *The Nature of Prejudice*
Albert Bandura's *Aggression: A Social Learning Analysis*
Hanna Batatu's *The Old Social Classes And The Revolutionary Movements Of Iraq*
Ha-Joon Chang's *Kicking Away the Ladder*
W. E. B. Du Bois's *The Souls of Black Folk*
Émile Durkheim's *On Suicide*
Frantz Fanon's *Black Skin, White Masks*
Frantz Fanon's *The Wretched of the Earth*
Eric Foner's *Reconstruction: America's Unfinished Revolution, 1863-1877*
Eugene Genovese's *Roll, Jordan, Roll: The World the Slaves Made*
Jack Goldstone's *Revolution and Rebellion in the Early Modern World*
Antonio Gramsci's *The Prison Notebooks*
Richard Herrnstein & Charles A Murray's *The Bell Curve: Intelligence and Class Structure in American Life*
Eric Hoffer's *The True Believer: Thoughts on the Nature of Mass Movements*
Jane Jacobs's *The Death and Life of Great American Cities*
Robert Lucas's *Why Doesn't Capital Flow from Rich to Poor Countries?*
Jay Macleod's *Ain't No Makin' It: Aspirations and Attainment in a Low Income Neighborhood*
Elaine May's *Homeward Bound: American Families in the Cold War Era*
Douglas McGregor's *The Human Side of Enterprise*
C. Wright Mills's *The Sociological Imagination*

Thomas Piketty's *Capital in the Twenty-First Century*
Robert D. Putman's *Bowling Alone*
David Riesman's *The Lonely Crowd: A Study of the Changing American Character*
Edward Said's *Orientalism*
Joan Wallach Scott's *Gender and the Politics of History*
Theda Skocpol's *States and Social Revolutions*
Max Weber's *The Protestant Ethic and the Spirit of Capitalism*

THEOLOGY

Augustine's *Confessions*
Benedict's *Rule of St Benedict*
Gustavo Gutiérrez's *A Theology of Liberation*
Carole Hillenbrand's *The Crusades: Islamic Perspectives*
David Hume's *Dialogues Concerning Natural Religion*
Immanuel Kant's *Religion within the Boundaries of Mere Reason*
Ernst Kantorowicz's *The King's Two Bodies: A Study in Medieval Political Theology*
Søren Kierkegaard's *The Sickness Unto Death*
C. S. Lewis's *The Abolition of Man*
Saba Mahmood's *The Politics of Piety: The Islamic Revival and the Feminist Subject*
Baruch Spinoza's *Ethics*
Keith Thomas's *Religion and the Decline of Magic*

COMING SOON

Chris Argyris's *The Individual and the Organisation*
Seyla Benhabib's *The Rights of Others*
Walter Benjamin's *The Work Of Art in the Age of Mechanical Reproduction*
John Berger's *Ways of Seeing*
Pierre Bourdieu's *Outline of a Theory of Practice*
Mary Douglas's *Purity and Danger*
Roland Dworkin's *Taking Rights Seriously*
James G. March's *Exploration and Exploitation in Organisational Learning*
Ikujiro Nonaka's *A Dynamic Theory of Organizational Knowledge Creation*
Griselda Pollock's *Vision and Difference*
Amartya Sen's *Inequality Re-Examined*
Susan Sontag's *On Photography*
Yasser Tabbaa's *The Transformation of Islamic Art*
Ludwig von Mises's *Theory of Money and Credit*